Customs and Tradition of China

中国的风气

穆 涛◎著

胡宗锋 【英】罗宾·吉尔班克◎译

河北出版传媒集团
河北少年儿童出版社
·石家庄·

图书在版编目（CIP）数据

中国的风气：汉文、英文/穆涛著；胡宗锋，（英）罗宾·吉尔班克译. — 石家庄：河北少年儿童出版社，2024.1

ISBN 978-7-5595-5683-7

Ⅰ.①中… Ⅱ.①穆… ②胡… ③罗… Ⅲ.①散文集–中国–当代–汉、英 Ⅳ.① I267

中国国家版本馆 CIP 数据核字（2023）第 073765 号

中国的风气
ZHONGGUO DE FENGQI

穆 涛◎著　　胡宗锋　［英］罗宾·吉尔班克◎译

选题策划：段建军　孙卓然	责任编辑：任立欣　金小力
美术编辑：孟恬然	封面设计：孟恬然

出版发行　河北少年儿童出版社
地　　址　石家庄市桥西区普惠路6号　邮编　050020
经　　销　新华书店
印　　刷　河北新华第一印刷有限责任公司
开　　本　880毫米×1300毫米　1/32
印　　张　6.25
版　　次　2024年1月第1版
印　　次　2024年1月第1次印刷
书　　号　ISBN 978-7-5595-5683-7
定　　价　32.00元

版权所有，侵权必究。
若发现缺页、错页、倒装等印刷质量问题，可直接向本社调换。
电话：010-87653015　传真：010-87653015

穆涛其人其事

贾平凹

我在《美文》杂志当主编,副主编是从河北石家庄调来的穆涛,他是个蛮有智慧又有一肚子谑趣的人。一天,我们驱车到外县去,经过秦岭北麓,他发感慨:"你们陕西人谦虚,这么大的山竟不称山,叫个岭。"我知道他又要作贱陕西了,就说:"说谦虚那比不上你们河北,那么大个省会不称城,叫个庄!"

车到一个山弯,忽然公路上奔跑着一只野兔,车一鸣喇叭,它就窜向路右边的半崖上,双耳翘起,小脑袋左右扭动,又跑下公路,竟在车前疾奔。车一加速,又一转身窜到左边的坡下,没想到跌了跟斗,一疙瘩毛肉滚将下去。穆涛就笑这野兔的机警,接着又说到老虎:"老虎之所以是老虎,它是没这份机警的,它总是慵懒地卧在那里,似乎在打盹儿,可一旦猎物出现,它一下子就捕获了,然后又卧在那里安安静静地什么也不作理。"

我说:"穆涛你说得好,我回去给你画张虎。"

穆涛说:"这可是你主动说的,你是君子!"

我说:"我当然是君子。"穆涛就快乐了,话也多得很,全说老虎的王者之气,最后他说:"你瞧瞧这汉语,词下得多准,给虎之前就加一个'老'字!"

我说:"是吗,鼠之前也加一个'老'字哩。"

从外县返回,我真的画了一张虎,画好了却舍不得再给穆涛。穆涛骂我画虎者有鼠气。

我说:"正因为有鼠气才把虎画留下要补虎气啊!"

因为喜欢了穆涛的文,也就喜欢了穆涛的人。人是小眼睛的,话又慢,仿佛在肚里酝酿了又酝酿,一点点地滴洒。

穆涛就占了个从容。

时下的国人依然浮躁着,但浮躁的文章人已经厌了。超越激愤,面对了永恒和没有永恒的局面,许多弄文的人忽然觉得从容就好,于是就从容,要么去写了鸡零狗碎的东西,要么如那些也要从容的书法家一样,偏把字写得松歪丑懒,其实一派造作。做人和做文,不是要从容就能从容的,它需要一种定力,定力又来自大的境界。穆涛的文有点儿像黄宾虹的画,以世界的角度来审视和重铸民族的传统,又藉传统的伸展或转移来确立自身的价值。

我并不知道穆涛的出身和经历,难以了解到他如此从容的原因。但我在研读了他的许多文章后,发现他的从容呈现出了他的一种文气和智慧。人是有聪明和智慧之分的。聪明的人到处都有,但聪明常常害人，要沦落到一个小字里边去；智慧却是难得，有智慧的人，特有一种艺术的感觉，平凡的事物里他会觉悟出非凡，话有三说，他巧说得有态有度，该肥就肥，该瘦就瘦，如美妇人。

文坛如社会，好人和坏人到处在平均分配着，尤其在当今，天才和小丑常常无法分清，闲人多多，投机者充斥。静观穆涛，他的心态十分健康。他似乎并不与人争一时短长，多于思考，博览群书，广泛吸收。想他眼小言慢，善于蓄力，就体会到了一句古语："口锐者天钝之，目空者鬼障之。"

穆涛从石家庄到西安，我们从作者与编辑的关系过渡到一个办公室的同事，开始了行立坐卧都很适意的生活。有茶清待客，无事乱翻书。人是有气味的，或许我们气味相投。

这么长的一部作品说了这么短一个序，如一个胖子头上的小帽，这帽子可以摘下不戴，权当是一本大戏开场前的几点锣鼓。

目　录 Contents

文化是有血有肉的 ·· 2
Culture has Blood and Flesh ·································· 3

坐船和吃饭 ·· 10
Sitting on a Boat and Eating ································· 11

内涵 ··· 18
Connotations ··· 19

局限 ··· 24
Limits ·· 25

道理 ··· 32
Truth ··· 33

表面的东西 ···································· 40
Superficial Things ······························ 41

"儒"这个字 ····································· 44
The Chinese Character for "Confucian" ········· 45

内装修 ··· 56
Interior Decorating ····························· 57

身体器官的服务员 ······························ 66
The Servers within the Organs of the Human Body ········· 67

回头看 ··· 74
Turning to Look Back ··························· 75

文明人 ··· 82
Civilised People ································ 83

去欲的态度 ···································· 88
Extirpating Desire ······························ 89

心中贼 ·· 100
Thieves in the Heart ·································· 101

代价与成本 ·· 110
Price and Cost ·· 111

立场与观念 ·· 120
Positions and Ideas ··································· 121

会说话 ·· 130
Knowing How to Talk ··································· 131

玉皇大帝住什么房子？··································· 140
What Kind of House Did the Jade Emperor Live in? ······ 141

写散文要说人话 ·· 158
To Write a Prose is To Say Human Words ················ 159

言者无罪：中国早期的民意调查 ·························· 172
Blame Not the Speaker: The Early Opinion Poll in China ··· 173

文化是有血有肉的

文化是活的。或者换一种说法,有生命力的文化,才会持久。梁漱溟老人给文化下过一个定义:"吾人生活所依靠的一切。"

怎么样理解这句话呢?

吃是饮食文化,吃后边有农业文化。穿是服饰文化,穿后边有工业文化。吃穿后边还都有商业文化。正在流行的叫时尚文化,已经过时的叫落后文化。居家是建筑文化,出行是交通文化,和平的日子有休闲文化,战争年月有军事文化,人们的生老病死是民俗文化。人的成长要接受教育,国家发展要靠科技,数典不忘祖是把根扎在传统文化里,一个民族在世界之林里真正的强

Culture has Blood and Flesh

Culture is alive; or, in other words, culture only endures for long if it possesses a life force. Liang Shuming once said that, "Culture is everything upon which our lives depend."

How to interpret this sentence?

Eating represents the culture of food, behind which there is the culture of farming. Dressing up represents clothing culture, behind which there lies the culture of industry. Behind eating and dressing up there is the culture of commerce. Whatever is popular is labelled "fashionable culture"; whatever is outdated is labelled "backward culture". Housing represents the culture of architecture; travel represents the culture of transportation; in peaceful times, there exists the culture of leisure; in wartime, there exists the martial culture; birth, ageing, growing sick, and death concern the culture of social customs. The

大还要开放着吸收外来文化。

一个人做事情的方式，是一个人的性格，叫个性。一个区域里的人做事情的方式，这种集体性格沉淀下来，就叫文化。

在我们中国，这种集体性格的差异是明显的，也是很具体的。生活在黄河流域和长江流域的人，衣食住行之间的差异很大。在黄河流域，陕西人、甘肃人、山西人是近邻，河南人与山东人是近邻，青海人和宁夏人是近邻，但近邻之间的集体性格差异很明显。在长江流域，湖南人和湖北人，江浙人和上海

cultivation of a man is dependent upon education, likewise, the development of a country is dependent upon science and technology. To be endowed with knowledge of all historic facts, including one's ancestors, is rooted in his traditional culture. The real greatness of a nation in a forest of world cultures is revealed by its openness to, and willingness to absorb foreign cultures.

The manner in which a man does things forms his character, that is to say his personality. Once the manner, in which a group of people does things collectively in a particular region, forms something like sediment, then it turns in to culture.

In China, the differences between collectives, with their own character, are both distinct and concrete. Those who live along the Yellow River and those who live along the Changjiang River exhibit great differences in their food, clothing, shelter and transportation. Along the Yellow River, the people of Shaanxi, Gansu and Shanxi are close neighbours; the people of Henan and Shandong are close neighbours; the people of Qinghai and Ningxia are close neighbours. Yet, even among

人，差异也迥然存在着。再往远处说，北京人和广东人，南辕北辙的差异更突出。

就陕西一个省而言，关中、陕南、陕北这三个地方的人差异也很大。在关中，西府人和东府人有区别；在陕北，延安人和榆林人有区别；在陕南，商洛、汉中、安康人也是如此。我们有两句涉及文化性格的老话，一句叫"十里不同俗"，一方水土养一方人。另一句话叫"喝一江水长大的"，这句话指的是不同的文化性格里还有相互融会贯通的一面。我们研究地域文化，既要看到相互区别的一面，还要寻找到相互融合，生发合力的一面。

these close neighbours the variation in their collective character is quite obvious. Along the Changjiang River, there are striking differences between the people of Hunan and Hubei, the people of Jiangsu and Zhejiang, and the people of Shanghai. If we go further, the differences between the people of Beijing and the people of Guangdong are even more striking.

As far as Shaanxi Province is concerned, there are great differences between the people of central Shaanxi, those of southern Shaanxi, and those of northern Shaanxi. In the central Shaanxi there are differences between the people of the west and the people of the east. In northern Shaanxi, the people of Yan'an and the people of Yulin are distinct. In southern Shaanxi, there are differences between people from Shangluo, Hanzhong and Ankang. There are two old sayings concerned with cultural personality. One is "Customs vary every ten *li*". A particular land nurtures particular people. Another saying goes "Grow up by drinking from the same river". This is referring to that, different cultures sport the façade of intermingling. When we study regional culture, we not only look for differences, but also seek mutual interactions and the power of combining these together.

中国的风气

一个地域的文化性格是一个地域的具体形象，是烙印一样的东西，想甩都不好甩掉，比如上海人的精细，东北人的粗犷。文化建设也是一个地域的形象建设，但这种形象建设不是一朝一夕或者"多快好省"可以干成的，也不是发了财，有了点儿钱，文化形象就光辉高大了。

我们中国自古以来就是"礼仪之邦"，各行当有各行当的规矩，"仁义礼智信"这些东西基本上是深入人心的。如今有两个自我检讨的热词："诚信缺失"和"信仰缺失"，其实都不太妥当，事实上是"规矩缺失"。

如今政府高调讲"繁荣文化"，我觉着首先应该对文化有个清醒的认识。

The cultural personality of a region is the specific image of a region. Like a marked brand which is indelible, such is the carefulness of the people of Shanghai, the directness and openness of the people of northeast. Cultural construction is the construction of a regional image. This image could not be achieved in a day or two through "more, faster, better, and cheaper" means. Neither does it mean that when there is money and fortune, the cultural image will become greater and more glorious.

China has long been labelled as the "Country of Rites". Every business has its norm. "Benevolence, righteousness, propriety, wisdom, and sincerity" are inherent in the hearts of everyone. Now there are two popular phrases for self-criticism: "lacking sincerity" and "lacking belief". Actually, these have not been properly stated. What is lacking is the norm.

The present administration has emphasized in a high tone the "prosperity of culture", but I think first things first, we should have a clear understanding of culture.

坐船和吃饭

读书像坐船。船有两种，一种是游船，一种是渡船。消遣书、休闲书是游船。坐游船的目的是休闲，是娱乐。坐渡船就很实际了，要有一个清晰的彼岸。如果你的目的地比较近，只是从河这边到河那边，这个船可以简陋一点儿，弄个竹筏都行。但如果你想跨过太平洋，或者远赴南极，这个船就复杂了，船体的结构要完整，船身质量要过硬，要抗得过台风。同时航海经验包括导航技术更要扎实，要确保能避过暗礁一类的危险。

Sitting on a Boat and Eating

Reading is like sitting on a boat. Boats come in two kinds—one is for recreation and the other is a ferry. Books intended for entertainment and leisure are akin to the former. Their purpose is to be uplifting and to offer joy. Taking a ferry is a practical exercise since one must be clear on where one wishes to go before embarking. Should the destination be close by, it might be a matter of crossing from one bank of a river to the other. The boat can be rudimentary in design with even a bamboo raft being fit for purpose. Nevertheless, if one wishes to cross the Pacific Ocean or voyage as far as the South Pole then the vessel must be far more intricate. The hull should be sturdy and shipshape enough to weather even a typhoon. Its experience including navigation technology ought to be sound in order to safeguard against dangers such as running aground on submerged reefs.

中国的风气

读书也像吃饭。

吃饭有两个目的,一是长身体,二是能干活。日常生活里的一些粗话指的是前者,如混吃等死、酒囊饭袋、吃货、饭桶、光吃不练。吃饭的主要目的是能干活。廉颇当年展示自己还能干一番事业的方式,就是多吃,在赵王派来的使者面前一口气吃了十斤肉、一斗米,然后提刀上马。但那个使者是被廉颇的对头贿赂过的,他回禀赵王说,老将能吃,但"一饭三遗矢"。廉颇将军奉献余热的心思就这么被终结了。

读书还要注意消化,不加选择地吃了一大堆,弄个消化不良会拉肚子,还

Reading is also like eating.

There are two purposes behind eating. One is to sustain the body, and the other is to provide fuel for labour. The former helps a person to get through each day. For instance, one can eat to kill time while awaiting death or treat one's body as a sack for wine or a bag for food, become a greedy gut and a bin, eating all the time while achieving nothing. The main purpose of eating is to be able to facilitate action. Lian Po, an old general in ancient times, demonstrated to others that he could still forge a great path by eating copiously. Before the eyes of the messenger from King Zhao he devoured five kilos of meat and about six kilos of rice. Afterwards he seized his blade and mounted his steed. And yet, the messenger had received a bribe from Lian Po's adversary before the visit. On his return he reported to King Zhao that the old general was an able eater, but "one meal called for three toilet breaks". Hence, Lian Po's autumn energy and desire were not allowed to be put to the service of his country.

While reading one must still pay attention to digestion. If an almighty heap is bolted down without discernment, a person

不如不读。

读书是充实自己，要能吃能干，读到肚子里的书要发挥作用。寺庙藏经阁里的虫子吃书多，而且吃的都是经典秘籍，但连身体都长不大，因此叫作书虫。郑板桥说过一段很有名气的话："学问二字，须要拆开看，学是学，问是问。今人有学而无问，虽读万卷书，只是一条钝汉尔。……读书好问，一问不得，不妨再三问，问一人不得，不妨问数十人，要使疑窦释然，精理迸露，故其落笔晶明洞彻，如观火观水也。"

might be left with indigestion and diarrhoea. Then, the outcome is worse than not being able to read in the first place.

Reading is meant to make one's self full. A person should be able to eat and to do things as well. The information learned from books should be applied to practical usage. The worms in temple studies and libraries have the capacity to gnaw at more tomes. Everything they eat is a classic or a specimen of arcane wisdom. Still, they cannot enlarge their bodies and are saddled with the monicker "bookworm". The eminent scholar Zheng Banqiao left behind the following well-known sayings: "Learning comprises studying and asking questions. Studying is studying and asking questions is asking questions. Nowadays people simply study without asking questions. Although they may have read thousands of books, they remain dumb articles. ... Reading consists of asking questions. If one cannot receive an answer the first time, persistence is necessary. If one person does not provide an answer, another person should be asked, and then a dozen and so forth until every doubt is assuaged and the knowledge gleaned has sunk in. Then the scholar can write with a crystal clear mind and the ease of gazing at fire or water."

中国的风气

让读的书发挥作用，也有两个指向。首先要改变自己的人生，"洞房花烛夜，金榜题名时"，古人这句话就是这层意思。把书读好了，中举人，做进士，得状元，荣耀门楣。但举人、进士、状元之后，真正的人生才开始，接下来要融入社会，要付诸实践，古人还有另外一个词，叫书生报国，要为社会和国家多做有益处、有功德的事情。

There are two possible directions by which to make use of what one has read. The first entails reforming one's life. An ancient saying—"A candle-lit wedding chamber and being listed on the imperial scholars' roll of honour."—conveys this very meaning. When one has learned much through reading, that is enough to pass the imperial examination and become a successful candidate at the provincial or national level, or even champion at the national level. That person can then bring honour to his family and clan. As a matter of fact, his life genuinely begins with this exam success. The second direction pertains to how the person must assimilate himself into society and put what he has learned into practice. Another ancient saying states that a scholar must return his debt to the country that nurtured him. He should perform profitable and virtuous deeds for the society and the nation.

内　涵

好的文章都内涵着情感。

春天，树在发芽之前，枝条先开始变柔软。或者换一种说法，冬天里的树落光叶子之后，枝条是僵硬的。这是我对情感在文章中存在形态的认识。

情感深沉着好，可以外露，但要由心底生出，且要自然而然。一篇文章里的情感如同一个人的情感，忌粉饰，忌矫情，忌虚伪，往肉里注水，增加了重量，但肉质坏了。

一篇文章没有情感，如同无情的人，让人躲着走。但情感要控制，要浓

Connotations

Fine articles are all imbued with emotional connotations.

In spring, before a tree is about to bud, its branches first become soft and supple. Correspondingly, in winter after the leaves of a tree wither, its branches turn tough and stiff. This is my understanding of how emotions should inhere within articles.

It is good that emotions run deep. They can lie on the surface, but should surge out naturally from the depths of the heart. The emotions in an article are the same as the emotions of a man. It is taboo to burnish emotions with powder, to display emotions coquettishly, or to be hypocritical about them. Each is like injecting water into a joint of meat. The weight may be enhanced, but the texture is spoiled.

An article without emotions is like a person who is devoid of feelings. People might shun them. However, emotions should

缩。情感讲究质量，不以数量取胜。家里有老人无常了，哭得厉害的，不一定是最孝顺的。情感怎么控制？谢灵运说得高远："升月隐山，落日映屿，收霞敛色，回飙拂渚。"

情感也要通俗，要有烟火气，要有常人的体温，要有人味。情歌都是通俗的，有些还庸俗，却有那么多人传唱。通俗不是肤浅，是被广泛受用。假惺惺的高雅、道貌岸然或装腔作势才是肤浅。伟大的情感这个词很特殊，是在特殊情况下，由特殊人物做特殊事业时体现出来的。伟大的情感不是生活常态，一个人身内身外全部是伟大情感，这不是人，是神。

be controlled and concentrated. Quality and not quantity should be the true yardstick. When an old man passes away, those members of the family who weep most profusely may not necessarily be the most filial. How should we control our emotions? Xie Lingyun said, "Like the rising moon hidden vaguely behind the mountains, like the setting sun shining on small and large archipelagoes, the solar glow of the dusk keeps its colourful glamour under restraint, and sweeps as a wild zephyr."

Emotions should also be earthy and bear both the flavour of kitchen smoke and the temperature and essence of humanity. Love songs are all earthy. Some of them are even vulgar. And yet, so many people adore singing them. To be earthy does not entail being shallow, but maintaining a style that is understood by the masses. Feigned elegance, pretended devotion, and fake airs are all symptoms of shallowness. Great emotion is a rarified expression. It denotes a special deed being performed by a special person under special conditions. Great emotions are not a part of daily routine. If a person were to be composed exclusively of great emotions from the inside to the outside, he

一个人爱父母,是天经地义,也是自私,因此要往开阔里写。爱山爱水爱花草树木爱身边的动物,是人之常情,但要写出新意,要挖掘出和别人不一样的东西。与众不同才叫别开生面。

真情实感是自然流露出来的。虚假的情感也装作自然流露,终究纸包不住火。西安有句土话:"听听哭丧的声音,就知道了谁是闺女,谁是儿媳妇。"

would not be a human being, but rather a deity.

It is right and proper for a person to love their parents, but this is also a form of selfishness. Thus one should put pen to paper with an open mind. To love the mountains, the waterways, flora and animals which surround us is a common emotional reaction. But one should write with a fresh creative spirit and disinter something different from others. To break virgin ground denotes that you are an unusual person.

True emotions flow naturally. That which is artificial also has its own natural flow, but paper cannot be used to wrap fire. A local saying in Xi'an says that, "In the mourning hall you can tell the daughter from the daughter-in-law." They weep in different ways.

局　限

有一个老话题，是宋朝人已经讨论过的，针对儒家的那句话："老吾老以及人之老。"说释迦牟尼和孔子有一天在河边探讨学问，两位的妈妈懒得听他们高深的理论，手拉着手去散步，走着走着，突然失足落水。佛祖静静地看着孔子如何行为。孔子讲礼数，不肯光着身子，和衣跳下水，先把自己的妈妈救上岸，再去救另一位老太太。这个话题应该是有佛心的人设立的，钻了儒门的空子。

据说中国民间有神通人，可以穿越时空，洞解人上辈子和下辈子的事。有

Limits

An old topic was discussed as far back as the Song Dynasty. It pertained to Confucianism: "Respect the elders in other families as you respect the elders in your own." Sakyamuni and Confucius were discussing academic matters on the riverbank. The mothers of the pair were not enamoured by their profound theorising and so went off for a stroll hand-in-hand. As they were walking, they suddenly and absentmindedly pitched headlong into a river. Sakyamuni watched on in silence to see how Confucius would react. Confucius knew the principle of rites. He was unwilling to undress, so leapt into the river fully-clothed. He first saved his mother and then the other elderly woman. This tale was actually concocted by a practitioner of Buddhism in order to pick holes in Confucianism.

It is said that there are people who can transcend time and space and relate what happened in past incarnations and

人问他："我上辈子是哪里人?"回答说："成都，西安，或呼伦贝尔大草原一带。"有美国人慕名学艺，学成后衣锦还乡，有人去请教："我下辈子脱胎去哪里?"回答说："底特律，俄亥俄，或科罗拉多大峡谷。"学术是没有国界的，这是有些做学问的人爱讲的一句话。术确实没有国界，手段可以通用，可以合营商业，可以联合军演。但比术再大些的，不仅有国界，甚至还有苛刻的地界。

山西万荣县有个故事，一个男子赶集回来对妻子说："我在半路上见到一个米袋子，捡起来一看，可惜开口在下边，底在上边。弄反了，拿回家也没用，就扔了。"妻子数落他："傻子，你把它拿回来，我把下边的口缝上，上边

foretell what will happen in future incarnations. Somebody asked one such person, "Where did I live in my previous existence?" The reply came, "Around Chengdu, Xi'an or the Hulunbuir Grasslands." An American who heard of this fellow's renown came along to learn from him. After he had served his apprenticeship, he went back home. Soon others approached him and enquired, "Whereabouts will I be born in my next life?" He answered, "Around Detroit, Ohio or the Grand Canyon." A saying among scholars states that academic learning knows no national boundaries. The same is true of technology. It can be applied universally to joint ventures and allied military drills. However, when the scope of the cooperation exceeds technology, dividing lines are apparent not only between nations, but are obvious among regions too.

A story from Wanrong County, Shanxi Province relates how a man returned from the local fair and said to his wife, "Halfway home I came across a sack for rice. Unfortunately, when I picked it up, the mouth was at the bottom. The opening was in the wrong place. I threw it away because it was useless." His wife then scolded him, "What a clot you are. If you'd brought it home,

再剪开口,不就可以用了。你个死心眼儿。"我觉着这不是笑话,是寓言。生活里学会换位思考是要紧的,学会怎样换位思考更要紧。

局限,是生活中的常态,普遍存在着。人的生死是局限,黑夜和白天是局限。左右手是局限,男女厕所是局限。春夏秋冬是局限,上下级是局限。一项体育竞赛,因为局限的存在,才会精彩。一件事情的发展过程,局限也是无处不在。息这个字的本意,是一呼一吸之间的停顿地带。气息,指的是呼吸再加上停顿的全过程。身体健康的人,既呼吸顺畅,停顿得也恰到好处。在大街上见一个人气息短促,如果不是遇到紧急情况,他的身体八成出现麻烦了。

I'd have sewn it back together and cut a new mouth in the top. Then we could use it, couldn't we? You're such a blockhead." I do not think this is so much a joke as a fable. In our lives, it is important that we should be willing to put ourselves in others' shoes. However, it is more important that we know how to put those shoes on.

Limits as a daily routine exist universally. Life and death are presented as limits, so too night and day, the left and the right hand, male and female conveniences, spring and summer and autumn and winter, senior ranks and junior ranks. A sporting event becomes more magnificent once we are aware of the limits imposed between competitors. Limits are also everywhere in all processes of development. The word "breather" in Chinese originally referred to the moment between exhaling and inhaling. "To breathe" denotes the entire process of expelling and consuming air and the intervening seconds. A healthy man knows how to exhale and inhale smoothly and when to pause in the middle. When we notice a breathless person out on the street, unless he has just been really exerting himself, his health may well be in grave peril.

中国的风气

做事情接连不顺利的人，俗话叫一步赶不上，步步赶不上，总是踩不到点上。那个点，就是局限的穴脉处。

Those who repeatedly fail in their enterprises must, to use a vulgar expression, be regarded as having missed the first step and buggered up their pace. Never again can they recover a sure and steady footing. That footing is the pulse of their limits.

道　理

　　道是讲理的，也是有自己的规律的。

　　道这个字，头在上，腿脚在下，思想与践行融为一体。空想，瞎琢磨，或本本主义，唱高调都不是道。低头拉车不看路，也不是道。每一条路都是有方向的，要用脑子去辨识。"摸着石头过河"不是硬道理，是特殊情况下的无奈举措，是心里没数时才使用的务实办法。我们中国人爱用走路比喻人生一世。"行路难"，是人活着不容易。"读万卷书，行万里路"，仅仅多念书不够，要经历世事，多加磨炼。还有坊间那句自吹自擂的话："我过的桥比你走的路多。"桥是路的断裂地带，是事故多

Truth

Truth (*dao*) has its own righteousness. And it also has its own regulations.

The shape of the character *dao*—道—consists of a head at the top and feet and legs below. In this single pictogram, thought and practice are fused into one. Utopian thinking, blind meditation, bookishness and lofty but hollow bragging do not belong to the way of truth. Nor does pulling a cart with one's head bowed, not looking ahead. Every route has its directions and one should judge according to personal discernment. "Crossing the river by fumbling along the stones" is not our top priority, but rather helpless measures in special conditions. This is a kind of practical method employed when one can be assured of nothing. We Chinese like to compare life to a stroll. When we say "the road is hard", that signifies that life is not easy. "Reading tens of thousands of books and walking tens

发区，是人生的麻烦处和要紧处，智慧者是在经过这种路况时才显出过人之处的。以前对皇帝有"明君"和"昏君"的判断，明君不是事事明了，而是对涉及国家命脉的大事摸得准，把得牢，拎得清。历史上有多位昏君，平常日子都明白着呢，只是每逢大事才糊涂。

人生卑微，不如草芥，草芥有根呢，枯了可再荣，年复一年葱茏度日。人没有根，死了就死了。如果不想一了百了，就多做些事情。人做事情就是给自己扎根，做大事，是扎深一点儿的根，根深，枝叶自然繁茂。青史驻名的

of thousands of *li*" means that book learning is inadequate. One should experience and practice more diligently. A popular saying boasts of how "I have walked more bridges than you have". Actually bridges are the fracture points of roads and the places where a great number of accidents occur. They also represent the critical junctures and areas of crisis in a man's life. The sages demonstrate their peerless wisdom as they encounter these very zones. In the past there reigned so-called "wise emperors" and "foolish emperors". The former did not necessarily view every matter in the empire with perspicacity, and yet were clear, precise and accurate when national survival was at stake. History is littered with so many foolish emperors. Their minds were lucid when it came to everyday affairs, but became addled when profound events were in sight.

Human life is more humble than a tuft of grass. Grass has roots. When it becomes withered it may yet be revived. This cycle is repeated year in, year out. People have no subterranean roots, so death is the end of our existence. If they wish to avoid this finality, they must strive harder for a legacy. To strive more represents the process of striking roots. The stronger their

那些大人物，就是把自己植根于世道人心里边了。

道貌岸然，是表面现象。道法自然，大道无形，指道的复杂和无量。但道不是虚无缥缈的，道是人间道，道的地基是常识，是寻常生活里过滤出来的认识和见识。

孔子多次在水边给学生上公开课，见到现实的场景，小题大做，展开他沧桑的心路。典型的有两次，一次是在波涛汹涌的河段见到一位"操之若神"的船夫，一次是见到激流漩涡里畅游的泳者。孔子用"轻水"和"忘水"点评船夫，"轻水"是了解水，掌握了水的性格才可以做船夫；"忘水"是和水打成一片，像鱼那样融于水。一条船翻了，

desire for greatness, the deeper their roots must penetrate. When a root reaches a more tremendous depth, the branches and leaves will naturally become more abundant and lush. Those famous figures whose names are engraved in history were each able to plant their roots in the hearts of the people.

Feigned devotion and eminence are something superficial. The great *dao* governs nature and is formless and hard to describe. This refers to the infinite and complicatedness of *dao*. However, *dao* is not entirely shapeless and illusive; it is the way of the world; the foundation of *dao* is common sense, and it is the understanding and insight filtered from daily life.

Many times Confucius gave alfresco classes to his disciples by the water's edge. Upon observing something insightful in nature, he would weave a far-encompassing exposition out of the tiniest trifle and unfold the vicissitudes he had experienced firsthand. There are two striking examples of this. One relates to how he once saw an oarsman "rowing calmly" along a choppy and turbulent river. The other concerns a swimmer merrily and gleefully negotiating whirlpools and eddies. Confucius applied the terms "belittling the water" and "forgetting about

落水的人可能惊慌失措，但船舱里的鱼有得水之乐呢。孔子向技艺高超的泳者提出问题，引导泳者沿着问题思路回答。泳者说："我是在水边长大的，在山靠山，在水吃水，慢慢地，水就是我的命了。"孔子得出的结论是，成就事业者，都是找到自己本命的人。

世道里有人心。孔子的自我评价是："吾少也贱，故多能鄙事。"这不是故意低姿态，是老僧的家常话呢。

the water" to explain the situation of the oarsman. "Belittling the water" means that in order to be an oarsman one must first understand the characteristics of water. "Forgetting about the water" means that you must fuse yourself into that very substance, much like a fish does. When a boat capsizes, those who are pitched into the water may very well panic, but those fish which have already been hauled in will feel overjoyed to be going home. Confucius posed some questions to the adept swimmer, which steered the swimmer to answering exactly how he wished. The swimmer said, "I grew up by the river. Those who live by the mountains make their livelihood from the mountains. Those who live by the river make their livelihood from the river. Gradually, the water became my life." Confucius concluded that: Those who can forge a great career are those who have discovered the substance of their own lives.

The way of the world is a matter of human mindset. Confucius commented on his earlier self that, "When I was young, my condition was low, and therefore I acquired an ability in many things, but they were mean matters." This is no understatement, but rather the household words of a sagacious old monk.

表面的东西

摆在表面的东西,多数不是真相,但也不一定是假象。

比如经过一片花生地、红薯地或土豆地,看到叶子绿油油的连成片,我们知道,果实是埋藏在下边的土壤里的。但透过枝叶的长势,我们可以判断果实的收成。在这样的状况下,枝叶和果实,共同构成着真相。

莲花开放在水面,藕隐身淤泥中。佛是爱莲花的,耳比芭蕉,心如莲花。但佛境界里的莲花不是世人眼中的莲花,也不在"出淤泥而不染"那个层面上。"孤舟蓑笠翁,独钓寒江雪",写的不是人的具体生活,而是精神世界里的真。这位"蓑笠翁"肯定不是靠打鱼为

Superficial Things

Most of the time what is displayed on the surface proves neither strictly true nor strictly false.

For instance, when you pass by a field of peanuts, sweet potatoes or regular potatoes, green leaves in bracts are on display. We know that the crops are buried beneath and through observing the foliage we can estimate the size of the harvest. In these circumstances, the leaves and the crops together constitute the fact of the situation.

Lotus blossoms open above the surface of the water. The roots lie hidden in the silt. The Buddha adores the lotus for his ears resembling plantain leaves and his heart the lotus flower. However, in the field of Buddhism, the lotus blossom is not the same as that in the eyes of ordinary people, nor does it evoke "rising from the mud unsullied". Liu Zongyuan wrote, "A lonely straw-cloaked fisherman afloat/ Is fishing for snow

生的人。真相、真知、真境界，这三个词，代表着三个指向，各有各的状态和高度。写文章的时候要留心，别把这三者混为一谈。

摆在生活的表面，一眼看上去就知道是假象的，不写也罢，写出来也难写出太大的意思。但苏轼有一节妙文，言短心长："僧谓酒为'般若汤'，谓鱼为'水梭花'，鸡为'钻篱菜'，竟无所益，但自欺而已，世常笑之，人有为不义而文之以美名者，与此何异哉！"

in a lonely boat." These two lines of poetry do not depict the concrete life of people, but rather the state of their spiritual world. The "straw-cloaked fisherman" is surely not somebody who makes his living by angling. True facts, true knowledge and a true spiritual world. These three expressions represent three alternative directions. Each of them has its own state and height. When one writes an article, care should be taken not to muddle the three into one.

One should not write about those things which are displayed on the surface in life or can be exposed as false upon first sight. Even if one tries to write about this, it is impossible to capture the breadth of the subject. The poet Su Shi coined several magnificent sayings, which are concise yet provocative: "Monks address wine as 'the soup of wisdom', fish as 'aquatic shuttle flowers', and chickens as 'fence hopping vegetables'. This is nothing but self-deception. Folks always laugh at such things. They can be said to be no different from those who write gaudy articles for unrighteous purposes!"

"儒"这个字

"儒"这个字的结构,一边是人,一边是需,内涵有两层意思,一是自己需要,再是被旁人需要。

一个人念书多了,有了学问,通了学理,去满足自己的需要,并有所斩获,叫自得。中举人,得进士,之后获赐一个好差使,都是自得。满腹经纶是说一个人有一肚子聪明才智。但如果受益人始终是自己,自得发展成了自私,局限就暴露出来了。即使是朋友之间往来,自私的人也是不受欢迎的。一个人发明了专利,自己领了专利费和荣誉证书,再有无数的人从专利技术中受益。儒这个字的内涵就圆满了。

The Chinese Character for "Confucian"

The shape of the Chinese character for Confucian—儒—consists of the image of a man on one side and the character for "need" on the other. It has two connotations: A man fills his needs, and he is needed by others.

When a man reads a great deal and accumulates learning, he is then capable of satisfying his own needs by understanding the principles of learning. He may also gain something for himself. This is known as "self-improvement". After he has attained the rank of first degree scholar or imperial scholar, he might occupy a fine position in the government. This is also a form of self-improvement. A brain full of learning denotes that the person's stomach is awash with wisdom and talent. However, if the profit is always withheld by the gleaner then self-improvement denatures into selfishness. His limits will consequently be exposed. The selfish find themselves

中国的风气

仅有书本知识不是儒,叫书呆子,或书虫。这两个词都形象有趣,知识是让人豁达和通达的,读傻了,成了呆子,是读拧了,读反了。书虫更生动逼真,在寺庙的藏经阁里,这种小动物很多,天天啃书,而且是经典秘籍,身体就是长不大,一个个满腹经纶,但那个腹实在有限。老百姓过日子有一句俗话,叫半大小子见风长。一个孩子吃母乳,喝牛奶,补多种营养品,父母的呵护到头了,到自己长个子的时候了。一个人长大成人,要沐风栉雨,不仅是生理的,还是心理的,更多的是社会磨砺而成的。一棵参天大树,不知经历过多少风雨,每生长一年,向上增高一点儿,树心也多出一个年轮。

unwelcome, even among good friends. When a man receives a fee and patent certificate for his invention then countless others gain dividends from his innovation. In this way the connotations of the word "Confucian" are fulfilled.

To possess only book learning is the preserve of the bookworm or reading fiend, not the Confucian. These two expressions are both vivid in their imagery. Knowledge makes people slick and broadminded. It is possible to become dumb through reading in an incorrect or contrary manner. The word "bookworm" is especially vivid. Those tiny animals abound in such number in the studies and libraries of monasteries and temples. They gnaw away at pages every day and even chomp down on classics. Even so, their bodies cannot grow larger. Each of their stomachs may be gorged with learning, though the capacity is indeed limited. A popular saying relates how "half-grown boys will shoot up as the wind gusts". A child may suck his mother's teat, drink milk, and consume various forms of nutritious product. When his parents judge that they have nurtured him enough, it is high time that he should take care of his own development. After a man has reached adulthood,

还有两个词，大儒和宿儒。大儒不是个子大，是影响广大，不仅被一个时代需要，而且要跨时代。《论语》是一本挺薄的书，但"半部论语治天下"，不停地被后世翻新沿用，汉代董仲舒翻新过一次，宋代朱熹翻新过一次，如今又被翻新着。中国在世界一百多所大学里建立了孔子学院，实在是了不起的大手笔。孔子是大儒，是天下读书人的老师，被累世尊奉着。

he must experience incessant wind and rain. These may be not only physiological, but psychological as well. What is more, he must endure social acclimatisation. When it comes to a tall tree that surges into the sky, it is impossible for us to guess how much wind and rain it has weathered. Each year when it grows taller, a new growth ring forms within its trunk.

There are two other noteworthy expressions. One is the "big Confucian". The other is the "venerable Confucian". "Big Confucian" does not mean that that person has a hulking frame. He must be a man who exerts influence. He is not only valuable to one era, but his worth transcends time. The *Analects* is in fact a slim volume. Nevertheless, the saying "half of the *Analects* is enough to govern the world" has been rediscovered and repeated by generation after generation. Dong Zhongshu rediscovered the book in the Han Dynasty and Zhu Xi did likewise in the Song. Now, it has been rediscovered once again. China has established Confucius Institutes in more than one hundred universities in the world. This really is a great advent. Confucius is a big Confucian, who remains the teacher of all those who read books under the skies and has been worshipped

宿儒也叫老学究，性格深沉，固执己见，"独善其身"的成分也偏多。纪晓岚写过两个老学究：一个信鬼的存在，一个不信，两个人争执了一辈子。信鬼的一个先死了，但坐在地府大门口死等，另一个终于来了，他拦着不让进门，严肃地提出一个问题："请说出你现在叫什么名字。"

在孔子的观念里，儒是综合能力。既有书本知识，更要有责任担当，且能做成事情。鲁国的季康子找孔子要人才，提名是子路、子贡、冉求。这三位都是孔子的得意门生，各有所长，但社会实践和综合能力不足。《论语》中的这段原文是：

by generation after generation.

A "venerable Confucian" can be addressed by the alternative title of "venerable scholar". Their personalities are profound and deep, and they insist upon their own understanding. Most of the time they adhere to the principle of "attending to one's own virtue in solitude". Ji Xiaolan once wrote about two such men. One believed in the existence of ghosts. The other did not. The two argued their whole lives long. The believer in ghosts passed away first, though he sat before the gates of hell and waited. Eventually, his counterpart joined him. He barred the way of the newcomer and posed an earnest question, "Please tell me now. What is your name?"

Within the philosophy of Confucius, "Confucian" refers to an integrated capability. One should possess both book knowledge and a sense of responsibility. Furthermore, that person should be accomplished enough to manage matters successfully. Ji Kangzi of the State of Lu approached Confucius and asked him to recommend individuals of talent. He listed the names of Zilu, Zigong and Ran Qiu. These three were the most beloved disciples of Confucius and each of them had his

中国的风气

　　季康子问：仲由（子路）可使从政也与？

　　子曰：由也果，于从政乎何有？

　　曰：赐（子贡）也可使从政也与？

　　曰：赐也达，于从政乎何有？

　　曰：求（冉求）也可使从政也与？

　　曰：求也艺，于从政乎何有？

　　这段精辟文字由六个问句构成，有智慧，有文法，这也是《论语》这部大书的文辞魅力的一种。

own areas of expertise. And yet all three fell short in social experience and integrated ability. The original description of this story in the *Analects* runs thus:

Ji Kangzi asked whether Zhong You (Zilu) was fit to be employed as an officer of the government.

Confucius said, "He is a man of decision; what difficulty would he find in being an officer of the government?"

Kangzi asked, "Is Ci (Zigong)fit to be employed as an officer of the government?"

And was answered, "Ci is a man of intelligence; what difficulty would he find in being an officer of the government?"

And to the same question about Qiu (Ran Qiu).

The Master gave the same reply, saying, "Qiu is a man of varied ability."

These brilliant words were formed through six questions, replete with wisdom and fine grammar. This accounts for part of the glamour of that great book, the *Analects*.

腐儒不是孔子的初衷，是臭豆腐，味道独出，也有叫人偏爱的一面，却上不了大席面。

To nurture bookish Confucians was not the original intention of Confucius. That type of person emerges like stinky tofu with its own unique flavour. They have their own taste for others to enjoy, but are not worthy to be presented at an official banquet.

内 装 修

我们的中医很了不起,用风和气的原理解释人的身体。

关于风和气,描述得最早,也最文学的是庄子:"大块噫气,其名为风。"风是无形的,我们走在旷野里,被风簇拥着,那是身体的感觉。"风吹皱一池春水",那是水的响应。风也是无声的,我们听到的声音,风声鹤唳,冷风嗖嗖,狂风怒号,是风碰到了东西,摩擦碰撞引发的动静。风碰到实的虚的东西,发出的声音是不一样的,有些如击鼓,有些如拿捏笛箫,有些如撩拨琴瑟,有些简陋的就是喇叭唢呐。庄子还发明了一个词,叫"吹万",世间万物

Interior Decorating

Chinese traditional medicine is really great. It employs the principles of wind and breath to explain the physiology of the human body.

The earliest and most literary description of the wind and breath appeared in the works of Zhuangzi, who explained that, "When the breath of the Great Mass of nature bears down strongly, it is called wind." The wind is formless. When we walk in the wilderness we are buffeted and encircled by the wind. That is the sensation we feel in our bodies. When the wind generates ripples in the pond, that is the aquatic version of an echo. The wind, moreover, has no independent sound of its own. The noises we hear which resemble crying cranes, the rustle of a chill breeze, and wayward squalls are the product of friction when the wind encounters a particular surface. The wind affects various sounds according to whether it meets a

的千姿百态,都是大自然这么"吹"出来的。

风协调着世间的万物。和谐了,则风和日丽,风调雨顺。风遇到梗阻,风云突变,就会出问题。小一点儿的问题如台风夹带着沙尘暴。大的问题如厄尔尼诺现象、拉尼娜现象,气候出现异常,大旱、大涝、酷暑、奇寒。"吹万"是大环境,大环境是人力不能左右的。有人类历史以来,大环境没有什么变化,日月星辰,风云雷电,大江大海,基本还是老样子,中间出现的局部问题,都是人类自酿的苦酒。

solid obstacle or a void. Sometimes it is like banging a drum, sometimes like producing a note from a flute, and sometimes like bowing violin strings. There are even times when it is as resonant as *suona* pipes being blown. Zhuangzi also coined another expression: "Blowing the myriad differences". All the various things in the world which differ in shape and state, were "blown out" by nature to assume their present form.

The wind adjusts every entity in the world. Where there is harmony, the wind is a mere breeze and the sun beams brightly. The onset of wind and rain comes in due course. When the wind is obstructed then the clouds and the wind alter abruptly. Danger may ensue. A milder instance of this may take the form of a typhoon or a sandstorm. More drastic ones may emulate El Nino or La Nina. The climate then becomes erratic, resulting in large-scale drought, floods, heat waves, and great chills. "Blowing the myriad differences" refers to the broader environment beyond the control of man. Since the dawn of mankind, the broader environment has scarcely changed. The sun, the moon, the stars, the winds, the clouds, the thunder and the lighting, the oceans and the seas have remained almost the

中国的风气

  我们每个人的身体，都是一个小地球，也可以叫小宇宙。一个人起早贪黑地忙碌，就是地球在一天一天自转。我们的身体被风内控着，意气风发，神清气爽，满面春风，甚至趾高气扬，都是风在体内运行正常的形态。风行不畅，麻烦就来了。风在"窍"处遇阻，会打嗝、放屁。风滞在经脉上，风湿、类风湿、关节炎，包括痛风这些病状就出现了。这些都是小麻烦，"中风"就复杂了，不仅仅是风行不畅，是风控制不了身体的局面了。中风的初级阶段头晕、眩晕、肢体麻木，高级阶段的恶果就不用我说了。

same as they were previously. The regional problems arising in history are all part of a bitter liquor distilled by mankind itself.

Everyone's body represents a microcosm of the earth or the cosmos. Each of us is busy from sunrise until nightfall. It is as if the earth has already completed an entire rotation. Our bodies are governed by the wind arising from inside. Whether one is in high spirits and vigorous, clear-minded and fresh, beaming with satisfaction, or even puffed up with pride, each of these states evokes the typical manner of the wind circulating within our bodies. When the wind cannot run its course smoothly, then troubles will arise. When it is obstructed in the "orifices", we may belch or suffer flatulence. Should it be blocked in meridians, this would give rise to diseases such as rheumatism, rheumatoid joints, arthritis and gout. These are all minor maladies, yet when a stroke hits matters become complicated. It is not then simply an issue of wind being unable to circulate with ease, but becoming powerless to control the functions of the body. In the early stages of a stroke, one experiences dizziness, vertigo and numbness in the limbs. There is no need for me to mention the insidious effects of the

中国的风气

　　一个老中医告诉过我一句顺口溜，"通则不痛，痛则不通"，指的就是风在体内的运行原理。

　　风和气不仅是生理的，还连着心理。喜怒哀乐是生理的，但和心理纠缠在一起。心安理得，心澄意远，也是这一层意思。生理和心理是"意识"的基础，说地基也行。意识的俗称叫念头。一个人从早晨醒来第一个念头算起，到晚上睡着之前最后一个念头（把"梦想"排除在外），一天之中要生出多少"杂念"？主动的，被迫的，潜意识的，下意识的，恐怕再细心的人也不便统计出来。这些念头串联在一起，一天又一天，一年又一年，人活一辈子活啥呀，就是活这些念头。万念俱灰是形容一个人活够了，活烦了。故此，儒家才强调明心见性，修身养性。道家不仅修心，

later stages.

A veteran doctor of Traditional Chinese Medicine told me a ditty, "Easy circulation causes no agony, and agony comes when circulation is not easy." This refers to the principles by which the wind circulates within the body.

The wind and the breath are not only physiological, but psychological phenomena. Happiness, anger, sadness and joy each have a physiological basis, but are intimately connected with the mind. Thus we say that a peaceful mind brings about contentment, while a mind made of pureness endows us with farsightedness. Physiology and psychology form the foundations or base of consciousness. A common name for consciousness is "idea". From the time when one wakes up in the morning and has the first idea of the day, until falls asleep at night after having had the final idea ("dreams" are excluded from this), how many "distracting thoughts" appear within one's mind? Some of these thoughts are active. Some are passive. Some are conscious, while others are unconscious. It is very hard to enumerate them, no matter how careful one is. When all of these thoughts are strung together, day after day and year after

连身子骨都修。儒和道两家都是围绕着一个人的"万念"去修，去粗取精，去伪存真。

修身养性是内装修，但内装修妥帖了，还要有所为。一个身心健康的人，如果一辈子碌碌无为，应该是最大的憾事。

year, they become the purpose behind a man's life. When we say that all hope has been dashed to pieces, it signifies that a man has had his fill of life and is bored with it. Hence, Confucianism emphasises the need for an enlightened mind and knowledge of one's nature. That is to say we must cultivate both the heart and nature. Followers of Taoism cultivate not only their minds but their bodies too. Both Confucianism and Taoism encourage the cultivation of the mind in spite of the vicissitudes of men's thoughts. By this means, the dross may be discarded and the essence refined, the false eliminated and the true retained.

The cultivation of the mind and nature is a form of interior decorating. When the process is completed, a man should also be left with the mindset to want to achieve something substantial. It is the greatest pity in the world that a man with a healthy mind and body should relentlessly fritter them away on worthless pursuits.

身体器官的服务员

大脑是受身体器官支配的。

饿了,要吃。渴了,要喝。寒了增衣,瞌睡了找枕头。腰酸了揉腰,腿麻了捶腿。憋屈了,出门走走,散散心。到年龄了,进小学中学大学,读硕士念博士,老话叫金榜题名,新名词叫为中华之崛起而读书。再到岁数了,娶个人或嫁个人,把婚姻大事办了。这些都是大脑的常务工作。

见到好吃的多吃几口,碰到漂亮的

The Servers within the Organs of the Human Body

The brain is manipulated by the organs of the human body.

When one is hungry one eats; when one is thirsty one drinks; when it is cold one puts on extra clothes; when one is sleepy one searches for a pillow; when a person's waist aches he massages it; when a person's leg is numb he pummels it with a fist; when one feels wronged and depressed one goes out to take a walk so as to lighten the heart. When the time comes one attends primary school, high school and then university. He strives for an MA and a PhD. In ancient times, this was called succeeding in the imperial examination. In the fashionable world of nowadays, it is known as "reading to bring about the rise of China". As more time passes, one gets married. Thus, one fulfills the conjugal obligation. All of these matters form the daily routine of the brain.

When one sees delicious food one eats a little more.

中国的风气

人多看几眼，遇着顺耳话多听几句。这是人之常情，但要守个度，不宜过量。人往高处走，芝麻开花节节高……这些都是励志的话，按着这样的图纸去施工的时候，大脑一定要清醒，不要被这些话弄得头昏脑涨，要留神这些话背后危险的一面。人做下了糊涂事，用西安土话说，叫脑子进水了。贪污犯，盗窃犯，强奸犯，杀人犯，脑子里不仅进了水，而且是涝了。

人的肚子里，窝藏着两种东西，食物和知识。这两样东西性质不同，但运行原理是一样的。都是以有形的模样，在大脑的统筹下收入"囊"中。饺子、面条、米、肉、蔬菜是食物，课本、书籍、榜样的行为是知识。之后消化成无形的能量，分散供给身体的各个器官。无法再消化的，就通过渠道排泄出去。

The Servers within the Organs of the Human Body

When one runs into a beautiful person one wants to have a double-take. When sweet words enter one's ears one wants to listen more. This is human nature. Even so, there should be boundaries which are not exceeded. People aspire to a higher position. As a sesame plant blossoms, it grows loftier and loftier... All of these are meant as words of encouragement. If one wants to follow these blueprints one must first have clarity in the brain and overcome all giddiness. One should be aware of the dangerous dimension behind these words. When one does something foolish, we call this "having water in the brain" in the dialect of Xi'an. Embezzlers, thieves, rapists and murderers not only have water in the brain, but their brains are truly flooded.

There are two entities hidden in the human belly: knowledge and what we have eaten. These two things are different in nature, yet conform to the same principle of circulation. Both have been consumed in a certain form or shape under the guidance of the brain. Boiled dumplings, noodles, rice, meat, and vegetables are food. Textbooks, books, and the deeds of those who set a good example constitute knowledge. After they have been digested and converted into

一个人把"之乎者也"吃进肚子，吐出来还是满嘴的"之乎者也"，就是没有消化好。读书和吃饭一样，不是越多越好，吃饱就行了。但吃饱了要去干活，这是吃的目的。一个人读了一肚子书，满腹经纶而无所作为，也是饭桶。

头悬梁，锥刺股，是古人发奋读书的两段掌故，是防瞌睡的苦肉办法。现代社会里这样的事少了，听的多的是割眼皮、垫鼻子、瘦腰瘦脸蛋不成功的医案。无论为了读书，还是为了美丽，这些方法均不宜提倡，精神升华到不给自己身体制造麻烦的程度为最佳。庄子写过三个残疾人，王骀、申徒嘉和哀骀它。前面两位没有小腿，是"兀者"。后边一位顾名思义，没脚指头，而且相

energy, this is distributed throughout the organs of the body. That which cannot be digested will be expelled through certain outlets. If a person eats "pearls of literary Chinese" and then expels them wholesale as the "pearls of literary Chinese", that means that they have not been digested properly. Studying is the same as eating. It is not a case of the more the better. As long as one is full that is enough. When one has eaten his fill he must return to work. That is the purpose of eating. If one has a bellyful of books and is possessed of learning and ability, but makes nothing out of this, he is just a bucket for food.

Tying their hair to the rafter and digging a bodkin into their thighs were two measures by which scholars in ancient times forced themselves to read attentively. These means of self-mortification prevented them from falling into a slumber. In modern society we hear less about these types of methods. What we hear more about are cases of failure, where people have sought unsuccessfully to have their eyes surgically enhanced or their noses lifted or their faces and waists made more slender. No matter whether the object is study or beauty, none of these methods should be advocated. The best recourse

貌丑陋。但这三位都是有大智慧的人，威震八方。王骀让孔子五体投地，申徒嘉让郑国宰相子产无地自容，哀骀它让鲁哀公心甘情愿献出王位。这三位智者的大脑，不是自己身体器官的好服务员，没照顾好身体的零部件，但它们实现了生命价值的最大化。这样的天赋人才也是极端的例子，读者不宜模仿。

The Servers within the Organs of the Human Body

is to elevate one's thoughts to such a degree that trouble is not brought upon one's own body. Zhuangzi once described three disabled persons. They were Wang Tai, Shentu Jia, and Aitai Tuo. The first two had no shins, so they were known as the "footless ones". The last one, according to the meaning of his name in Chinese, had no toes and was grotesque. However, these three were all great minds. Their fame spread far and wide. Wang Tai made Confucius prostrate himself before him. Shentu Jia made the Prime Minister of the Kingdom of Zheng, Zichan feel ashamed to show his face. Aitai Tuo made Duke Ai of Lu willingly offer his throne to him. The brains of these three great minds were not good servers to the organs of the body. They did not take diligent care of all the parts of the body, yet they realized the value of life to its full potential. These talented people were extreme examples. Readers are not prepared to imitate them.

回头看

写历史题材的文章是回头看。

回头看,要有历史观。历史观,就是以什么样的眼光和立场看待前朝的人和事。

前朝差不多都是被推翻的,这是我们中国历史上下朝代之间的基本关系。朝代更替,轻松着说,叫翻开了崭新的一页,但翻动这一页的手指头一点儿也不轻松,是撕破了脸,大骂大砍大杀,老百姓都要经历数不尽的血雨腥风。我们的历史是断代史,被割裂为二十五个自然段落。有一个比喻说中国历史是一条长河,还要补充一句,这条长河上有

Turning to Look Back

Writing articles on the theme of history entails turning to look back.

In order to be able to turn to look back, one first requires a conception of history. By "conception of history" we mean examining themes and people in bygone dynasties according to our viewpoint and position.

Almost all of the bygone dynasties were overthrown by another. This forms the basic relationship between regimes in Chinese history. The replacing of one dynasty by another, if put in a lighthearted way can be called "turning over a brand new leaf". However, the finger which turned over that leaf was far from lighthearted in spirit. All considerations of face had to be put aside, together with feuds, murders and slayings, and ordinary people suffered through endless gales of blood. Our history is a dynastic one, which has been sliced into twenty-

二十四座截流大坝。这些段落是被政治的手术刀切割开的，进行段落连接的是文化传统。政治与文化，在这种节骨眼上就是这么分工合作的。

用今天的眼光看，重视朝代之间衔接和传承的皇帝，都是明君。元朝在这一点上没有做好，他们比较忽视和亡宋的衔接，更忽视中国文化的血脉传统。元朝初年，地方官有半数以上甚至不懂汉语，要带翻译。团结以及振奋民心的工作主要通过各种歌舞戏曲集会，这一点也帮了中国文学史的忙，元曲成为元代文学的制高点。歌舞戏曲成为文化主航道的朝代，是浪漫型的，但从根子上说，执政的人不太熟悉中国历史。清朝也是少数民族掌握国家大政，他们汲取教训，高度重视文化的传承与融合，具

five natural portions. There is a simile which likens Chinese history to a long river. One clause should be added to this. Along the course of this long river there are twenty-four dams. These portions were sliced up by the scalpel of politics. What unite these severed portions are cultural traditions. Politics and culture share the work and help each other at these crucial junctures.

In the eyes of today, the emperors who paid sufficient attention to the legacy and the transitions between former dynasties are the so-called "diligent emperors". The Yuan Dynasty did not perform well in this respect. Its leaders neglected to scrutinize the juncture between it and the overthrown Song Dynasty. More significantly, they neglected the tradition of blood lineage. In the early years of the Yuan Dynasty, more than half of the local officials did not even understand Mandarin. When meetings were held interpreters were required. The work of uniting and encouraging the hearts of the people was mainly reliant upon various song and dance spectacles, as well as operatic events. Nonetheless, this also stimulated their contribution to the history of Chinese

体做的事情有许多,其中之一是整理出版了三套了不起的大书:《康熙字典》《古今图书集成》《四库全书》。这三套书,用今天的政府话说,都叫重点文化工程。

回头看,是为了更好地向前走,因此清醒是至关重要的。没有正向感而寻求反向,会从现实的泥淖滑入历史的漩涡。

立场,是观察者从什么角度去看

literature. The Melodies of the Yuan Dynasty became the apogee of culture then. When song, dance and opera became the main channel for culture in a dynasty it could be said that this dynasty was romantic, but from looking back to the roots of this we can observe that the administrators were not familiar with Chinese history. The Qing Dynasty was also controlled by an ethnic minority. They drew lessons from the previous dynasties, paid great attention to the inheritance and fusion of culture. They conducted many specific projects. One of them was to sort out and compile three great books. They were *Kangxi Dictionary*, *Collections of Books in Past and Present*, and *Complete Library in the Four Branches of Literature*. To use the words of the present administration, these three great books are the "key cultural projects".

In order to walk forward in a better way one needs to turn to look back. It is vital to keep a clear mind. Where there is no positive sense of purpose one searches instead for a negative sense of purpose and thus we will slide from the mire of the present to the whirlpool of history.

Position means the angle through which a person looks

问题。有一个真实的例子，是平凹主编和我闲聊时说到的。在贵州某处的一个小山村，一户人家的儿子考取了重点大学，又念完了博士，留在北京工作，儿子很孝顺，常接父母去住，但每一回都要反复做工作。村里人问老汉："北京不好么？"回答说："好是好，就是太偏僻，去一回要走好几天的路。"

写历史散文，盲人摸象和坐井观天会失之偏颇。"白头宫女在，闲坐说玄宗"那一种，又过于伤流年。戏说或信口开河地说，作为娱乐可以，当正经文学事去干，也不太妥当。

at a problem. There is a true example of this. When we were chatting, Jia Pingwa, the Editor-in-Chief of our magazine, told me that in a tiny out-of-the-way village in the deep mountains of Guizhou Province, the talented son of a poor family was granted admission to a key university. After he completed his PhD he was assigned to work in Beijing. The son was a very filial individual. He invited his parents to live in Beijing, but time and again he had difficulty persuading them. The villagers asked the old man, "Beijing is not good, is it?" He answered, "Beijing is really good. It is just that it is too far out-of-the-way. It would take several days to get there."

The writing of historical prose is biased in that one follows either the way of the blind man who touches the elephant or the frog who sits at the bottom of the well. A Tang Dynasty poem states, "The white-haired lady-in-waiting is still alive,/ She talks idly about the Xuanzong Emperor." This kind of record would be too sentimental. Talking about history in a playful or random way is only acceptable for entertainment. It is not proper to take it as a serious literary mode.

文 明 人

　　一片遥远得惊人的土地上，草木繁茂，香花灿烂，石头们各具形态地静立着，水含光放波地流动着，飞鸟和走兽心存爱意地彼此相生相克着。一天，来了两个能人，有能耐的男人和女人，没有谁知道他们因为什么或为了什么来到这里，事实是他们来了，砍伐树木，建起了第一所房子。收割禾草，燃起了第一缕炊烟。为了活着，他们开始适应这块土地。一年之后，他们的孩子出生了，渐渐地，又有路人在此落草定居。多少年后，人烟变得稠密了。一些惊慌失措的野兽被驯服，变为家禽私畜。另一些有主见的野兽在人们的武器和篝火的包围下或灭绝或远远地遁去。

Civilised People

In a surprisingly remote land, the grass and trees grew densely and vigorously. Fragrant flowers were in full bloom, rocks and stones of various formations stood inanimate, and water rippled, shimmering with light. Soaring birds and charging animals were part of the same food chain, but these carnivores were neighbours as well as predators. One day two capable folk—a man and a woman—came along. No one knew why they chose this place and for what purpose. The fact is that when they arrived they felled the trees and built the first ever house here. The pair mowed grass to generate the first kitchen smoke. In order to survive, they had to adapt to this region. One year later, their child was born. Gradually, other travellers began to settle hereabouts. Many years later both the population and the smoke had mushroomed. Some wary wild animals were domesticated and became household livestock.

中国的风气

  人们越聚越多，杂草灌木丛林被烧伐着，迅速向后退去，房屋与房屋之间出现了街道，街道与街道相连或相错，相继有了学校、商店、邮局、银行、交易市场、贸易大楼以及行政管理大楼，至此，这片土地被命名为"城市"，人们开始觉得生活在城市里就是文明人。

  然而，多年之后，城里人越来越多，楼房取代了平房，而且楼层越来越高，汽车取代了骡马，而且汽车越来越豪华，城市越扩越大，人们求生存的本领也越来越高超，这时候出现了一个词汇——环境污染。人们面对着自身的浮躁与不安，以及各种传染疾病，开始想念当初的原始风景了，每到休息日便到田野山间度假，回到家里又养了花，门前植了树，建筑家们在拥挤的交叉路口

Other more headstrong beasts were killed by or fled afar from man's weapons and the heat of the flames.

The population burgeoned. Grass, bushes and forests were torched and the bounds of the vegetation receded rapidly. Streets unfurled between residences, crisscrossing and bisecting one another. Then schools, shops, post offices, banks, outdoor markets, trading mansions, and administrative blocks materialised. Not until now did they name this piece of land the "city". It then became the standard view that those who lived in the city were civilised people.

However, years later the urban population had increased yet further. High-rises had replaced single-storey buildings, jutting relentlessly into the skies. Mules and horses had been superseded by automobiles which became more and more luxurious. The city had dilated to an unprecedented scale. People's survival skills had become more acute. At this stage, the expression "environmental pollution" entered the vocabulary. In the face of their own turbulence and unease, in addition to a plethora of infectious diseases, folks began to yearn for the original primitive landscape. On weekends

建了街心花圃，在街道两侧铺垫了草坪，甚至别出心裁地在高耸的大厦顶层设计了空中花园。发了横财但求心安的企业家远去非洲或美洲的原始部落，以高价收买早年被驱逐走的飞禽走兽，放进城市的动物园里，使之与孩子们维持着几米栅栏的隔阂。有一天，某人用高科技的猎枪在郊外打死一只野天鹅，整座城市的报纸和电视众口一词地咒骂："野蛮！不文明！"

文明，差不多总是在前面导引着我们，有时候却也绕到身后，类似黄昏时分仍没回家的孩子所听到的妈妈站在门口发出的严厉又焦虑的一声声呼唤。

and red letter days, they would head for the mountains and meadows for recreation. What is more, they sowed flowers at home and planted saplings out front. Architects designed efflorescent traffic islands to plug the teeming crossroads and turfed over both sides of the street. They even invented the bespoke rooftop garden to perch at the summit of the tallest skyscrapers. In an effort to un-sully their consciences, the nouveau riche entrepreneurs sought out the primitive tribes of Africa and America. They spent a fortune purchasing the soaring birds and charging animals their predecessors had driven away, and placed these specimens in the municipal zoo. Fences penned off the captive creatures from visiting children. One day, someone shot a wild swan with a high-tech rifle. All the newspaper readers and TV viewers in the city cursed the miscreant in unison, "Barbarian! So uncivilised!"

Civilisation almost always leads us as the vanguard. Nevertheless, it sometimes creeps to our rear like a mother who stands at the entrance to the home calling out earnestly and anxiously for her kids when they haven't returned at dusk.

去欲的态度

欲是好东西,让人生有意义。

自然而然是欲,饿了吃饭,渴了喝水,寒了增衣,困了放松,瞌睡了找枕头。由平庸到高尚,由常人到伟大,是欲在发挥作用。但欲是有界限的,煮饭的是火,火过头煮糊了,或烧了厨房,是超限,是越界。中国的皇帝有伟大的一面,也有自私卑鄙的一面。比如太监这个职业,以前,在"中央机关"内部从事服务工作的男子要被阉割。陕西土话把阉割叫去势,这个词真是形象到位,把人的根本东西拿掉了,有形无势,无法形势大好。太监是皇帝的私欲延伸的恶果,如果皇帝和普通人一样,只娶一个老婆,太监的形势就保全了。

Extirpating Desire

Desire is a positive force; it endows life with significance.

Desire is natural. When hungry you eat; when thirsty you drink; when the weather being cold you put on extra clothes; when overcome with tiredness you allow yourself a rest; and when exhausted you seek out a pillow. From commoners to nobility, from the humble to the exalted, desire is the driver. But desire also has its boundaries. In the process of cooking a meal, if the fire rages too fiercely the food will be scorched or the kitchen might even be engulfed in a blaze. This is surpassing the safe boundaries and limits. Chinese emperors had their magnificence, but they also had their selfish and despicable side. Take for example the profession of a eunuch. In ancient times, those men engaged in the central government civil service were compelled to be castrated. In Shaanxi dialect we call this "tearing off power" (*qu shi*). This expression is graphic

中国的风气

"养生难在去欲",是苏轼的一句名言。树长成栋梁要剪枝,平头百姓跃为大人物要去欲。皇帝是该带头去欲的,普通人的欲火烧自身,为所欲为的皇帝烧的可是整个国家。人去欲是难的,去掉哪些?去掉多少?不好把握。猪八戒是什么都不戒的,因而是个笑柄。和尚剃光头发,把头顶的、心里的全部去掉,放弃现实的人生,是难为人,特殊材料制成的人才能做到。让皇帝去欲,更难。千辛万苦地成了皇帝,我容易吗!电视剧《康熙王朝》有一句主题歌词:"我真的还想再活五百年。"他是皇帝,肯定想活五百年,正受熬煎的老百姓,肯定就不这样想了。

and direct. Remove the fundamental aspects of a man and you reduce him to a shell devoid of vitality. His figure and force could not be described as winsome. A eunuch is the maleficent seed of the emperor's overblown desire. If the emperor, like ordinary men, only married one wife eunuchs could surely be allowed to retain both their figure and their force. The poet Su Shi famously said, "The toughest task in life is to curb one's desire." The branches of a tree must be pollarded if it is to develop a sturdier trunk. When a normal person gains eminence, he should be swift to restrain himself. Emperors ought to take the lead in managing their desire. Common folk only singe their own fingers with desire, yet the monarch's desire can set the whole country alight. Curbing desire may be tough, and what kind of desire should be curbed? And to what extent should it be curbed? This is troublesome to determine. The character of the Pig in *The Journey to the West* curbed none of his desires. Hence he became a laughing stock. A monk shaved his head, uprooting what was on his head and in his mind. He turned his back on worldly life. That is onerous. Only men of a particular disposition can achieve that. It would be

中国的风气

　　人生一辈子,寿限大约一百年,性子急的少一些,肠子宽的略多一些。老天爷的这个设置是有大局观的,一个人活到六七十岁,把人生的基本东西看透了,但活明白了就退休了,只好把"人生经验"传递给下一代。这个节骨眼上,老天爷又加装了一个"代沟"的装置,孩子不吃老子那一套,所有的事情要重新来过,吃二遍苦,受二茬罪,把人生的跟头再重新跌一圈。"代沟"是符合科学发展观的,预防人类进化的步子迈得太快。试想人生是三百年,退休制度是二百六十岁,街上走的,屋里坐

more difficult still for an emperor to curb his desire. He might say, "I tried my best to get to where I am. Was that a walk in the park for me?" One episode of the TV serial *The Emperor Kangxi* features a song which states, "I really want to live for another five centuries." He was the emperor so was bound to harbour this aspiration. As for the suffering masses, they surely would not think so.

A human lifespan may not exceed one hundred years. Those with a hasty temperament might be short-lived, whereas those with a strong stomach might prolong their existence. The heavens weigh up every factor when ordaining the number of our days on earth. A man of sixty or seventy has weathered almost every conceivable circumstance. Once he has seen through them all, he is obliged to retire. His "life experience" must be bequeathed to the next generation. At this critical juncture, the heavens engineer a new phenomenon in the chain of being, known as the "generation gap". The younger folk rebuke the lessons of their elders. They are apt to explore every situation for themselves, suffering and enduring the same tribulations as their predecessors. The somersaults of life

的，多数是人精，人种可能延续不到今天，早灭绝了。从这个角度看，老天爷也是在去欲，但成就的是天大的事。

"人间随处有乘除"，这是曾国藩诗里的一句。曾国藩不是大诗人，写的多是哲理诗，在哲理上也比苏轼差一个档次。但苏轼不会带兵打仗，也不会经营自己的人生，诗词文章一篇比一篇好，但做官是一年比一年小，贬了再贬。苏轼属于虚高一等，在人生层面上，去欲稍多了些。王维呀，白居易呀，又会写诗，又会做官，活的年头也长，鱼和熊

have to be rehearsed from scratch. The generation gap concurs with the Scientific Outlook on Development as it serves to prevent the rate of human evolution accelerating too fast. Let us imagine if humans had a life expectancy of three hundred years with two hundred and sixty set as the retirement age. Most of the people who walk out on the streets or sit at home would be ghostly shells. The human race could not have persisted until now. It would have long ago been consigned to extinction. From this perspective, we can see that the heavens too are at pains to curb their desire. In limiting our mortal lives to a more modest span, it has enacted its own stroke of genius.

"At any point there is multiplication and division in life." So goes a line from a poem by Zeng Guofan. Zeng was not a master poet and most of his verses are philosophical in character. His poems of ideas cannot hold a candle to those of Su Shi. Nonetheless, Su Shi had no knowledge of combat or of leading military forces, nor could he take control of his own life. His poems improved exponentially as he went along, in diametric opposition to his lot as an official. He was repeatedly exiled and so belonged to that group of people who defy the logic of

掌都得了。

"人为财死，鸟为食亡"，居家过日子一点儿一点儿积累财产，由温饱到小康，是做加法。一夜暴富的人，是做乘法。在秩序井然的社会里，做加法的人多。在少规则的年月，做乘法的人多。乱世出英雄，就是这个意思。乱世，不仅指战火硝烟，百姓流离失所。繁荣的社会缺少章法，至少不能叫政治澄明。

做除法，先从减法做起。减法也难做，钱越多越好，名越重越好，官帽子越大越好。一个人从"闻鸡起舞"到

metaphysics. In the sphere of human desires, he demonstrated a shred of self-control. By contrast, Wang Wei and Bai Juyi struck a balance between creative effulgence and an aptitude for office. Consequently, they were blessed with long lives and could savour the whole gustatory gamut from fish to bears paws.

Men die from seeking a fortune and birds are killed for the plate. Family life encompasses the patient accumulation of property. From being adequately clothed and fed to being fairly well-off, is a basic process of addition. Those who strike gold overnight are working miracles of multiplication. In an orderly and systematic society, addition is the main arithmetical stratagem. In an era of disorder and chaos, multiplication takes over. This is the meaning of the saying "a chaotic world breeds heroes". A chaotic world not only refers to one riven by war and skirmishes, where the populace has no sanctuary. If a prosperous society lacks order and system, it cannot claim that its politics are transparent and well-defined.

When we are undertaking division, we take subtraction as our starting point. Subtractions are also arduous. As for money, the more the better. As for fame, the greater the better. As for

"戴月荷锄归",每天起早贪黑地忙碌,都是围绕着"钱、名、官"这三个字转。等到有一天累病了,躺在床上,心里才恨着骂这三个字竟无半点儿用处。但身子康复了,又上路去旋转了。

有一个老掉牙的故事,说一个临死的财主,连着几天合不上眼皮,还高举着两个手指头,儿孙们百思不得其解。老伴相知一生,将燃着的两个油灯头,吹灭了一个,财主才放心地撒手尘寰。这样的人实在可恨又可爱,真真地是把一个事业进行到底了。

one's official position, the higher the better. A man "rises with the cock's crow" and "returns shouldering a hoe under the moonlight". Those three expressions—money, fame and official position—keep him occupied from dawn to nightfall. Until one day he succumbs to fatigue and cannot get out of bed, he will then curse that this trio is useless in his heart. Anyhow, on making a mild recovery, he again sets out in pursuit of them.

An old chestnut relates how an elderly landlord nearing death could not close his eyes for several days, yet was able to raise two fingers. His children and grandchildren could not make out what he was trying to communicate. His wife, having been his lifelong companion, promptly blew out one of their two oil lamps. The landlord then lowered his hand and passed away. This kind of person is both loathsome and endearing. He truly carried his life's preoccupation right up until the very end.

心 中 贼

"破山中贼易,破心中贼难",这是大学问家王阳明说的。

他这话真是说到点子上了,虽说人心都是肉长的,但这块肉实在是博大精深,复杂无限。比天高,比地厚,比海深,比火热,比金贵,比冰凉,比铁硬,比纸薄。世态千万般的演化变故,发祥地和归宿地全在这块肉上。有一副老对联,说的也是这层意思:"百善孝为先,原心不原迹,原迹家贫无孝子;万恶淫为首,论迹不论心,论心世上少完人。"

Thieves in the Heart

"It is easy to capture thieves in the mountains, but not the thieves in your heart." So wrote the great philosopher Wang Yangming.

His words are rather to the point. Even though the human heart is made of flesh, this piece of flesh is expansive, refined and inscrutable. It is loftier than the sky, thicker than the earth, deeper than oceans, hotter than fire, more precious than gold, chillier than ice, tougher than iron, and thinner than a leaf of paper. Every single change in the world has its origin and resolution in this piece of flesh. An ancient couplet describes this thus—Among the hundreds of varieties of goodness, filial piety ranks the first; it is revealed through the heart rather than works; otherwise poor families would be utterly bereft. Among the hundreds of varieties of evil, obscenity ranks the worst; it is revealed through works rather than the heart; otherwise there

中国的风气

心中贼是原罪。佛门称恶念，由恶念生成十恶业，杀、盗、淫，这是身体上的。妄语、绮语、两舌、恶口，这是嘴上的。贪、嗔、痴，这是心里的。多年前，平凹主编在书柜上写过八个字："群居防口，独坐防心"，这几天西安雨水勤，房子又在漏雨，早晨去看他的办公室，这八个字依旧新鲜。

纪晓岚写过两种心中贼。一个富婆叫张太夫人，养着一条小花狗，张太夫人岁数大了，狗由几个丫鬟带领着，平安和谐地过日子。故事由厨房的肉总是丢失开始，丫鬟们怀疑是小花狗偷吃的，集体做出了一个决定，把小花狗私下里杀了。这件事过去几天了，却一直过不去。有一个丫鬟叫柳意，一个很漂

would be few perfect men left.

Thieves in the heart are the original sin. In Buddhism this is known as "evil intentions". These include murder, robbing and obscenity and are all concerned with the body. Lies, profane words, having a forked tongue, and swearing are all concerned with the mouth. Greed, anger, and addiction are all concerned with the mind. Many years ago, Jia Pingwa wrote out eight characters on his bookshelves, "Bridle your mouth socially. Bridle thoughts in solitude." In recent days, Xi'an has seen constant downpours. Houses have been leaking. When I went to inspect his office in the morning, those eight characters remained fresh and striking.

The Qing Dynasty official Ji Xiaolan delineated two types of thieves in the heart. One was a rich lady by the name of Madame Zhang. She kept a spotted lapdog. As she was long in the tooth, she asked several of her housemaids to look after it. Life wore on peacefully. The story proper began with the regular disappearance of meat from the kitchen. The maids suspected that the dog was the culprit, so made a pact to secretly kill it. Several days after the deed was done, it still cast a shadow over

亮的女生,她每天晚上做噩梦,梦到那条小花狗在追着咬她。张太夫人知道情况后,说了一番很有水平的话:"群婢共杀犬,何独衔冤于柳意,此必柳意亦盗肉,不足服其心也。"把柳意叫过来审问,果然如此。恶是隐不住的,我们的传统观念不仅憎恶,对隐恶更憎。

第二位是一个老学究,旧说法叫宿儒。一天夜里,无常鬼来捉他,他以为寿限到了,就跟着走,到地府销生死簿的时候,才知道抓错了人。老学究大义凛然,要求拨乱反正,不依不饶的,还要追究责任。城隍是地方法官,给他赔礼道歉,杖责无常鬼二十棍。老学究素有得理不饶人的声名,如今鬼也不肯轻饶。最后首席大法官阎王爷出面了,才马马虎虎地把这件事了结。阎王爷

them. One of the girls, a beauty called Liu Yi, was afflicted by recurrent nightmares. In her dream the dog was chasing after her and sinking its teeth into her flesh. When Madame Zhang learned about this, she shared a pearl of wisdom, "You maids conspired together to slay a pet, but why is only Liu Yi plagued with guilt? Obviously, she was the actual meat thief. The animal realised the injustice of it all." Liu Yi was hauled over for cross-examination. It turned out that the allegation was correct. Evil cannot be hidden. According to traditional concepts, evil is to be disliked, but hidden evil is to be totally abhorred.

The second story relates what happened to an aged scholar. In ancient times, a scholar was known as a "learned Confucian". One night the God of Death sent his henchmen over to capture him. Believing that his days had come to an end, he followed them. On reaching hell and examining the Book of Life and Death, they discovered that they had captured the wrong person. Fearlessly, the aged scholar demanded this aberration be rectified. The City God, who was the local presiding judge, expressed his apologies and commanded that the henchmen be lashed with twenty rods. The aged scholar

中国的风气

劝他："事情是糊涂鬼做出的，是疏忽，也没造成严重的后果，又不属于人间官府的存心害人，您老人家高抬贵手吧。'夫天行不能无岁差，况鬼神乎？'"在阎王爷那里，心机正邪是判断一件事情的重要标准。

这两天还听说了一件新鲜事。一个有钱的医生办了一家公司，请他的中学同学做董事长，这董事长是虚职，不用上班，年薪五万。这位同学流年不顺，又下了岗，正在家里恓惶着数日子，见天降及时雨，以为人到中年改了运程，铁树要开花了，千恩万谢地接了证书，并且逢人就夸誉老同学："整座城里就

had long enjoyed a reputation for not forgiving people even when they admitted their guilt. Even in the depths of hell, he would not show mercy to these spirits. Duly, the chief justice, the God of Death, came along to settle the matter. He said, "The muddleheaded henchmen are to blame for your manhandling. Their absentmindedness caused this. No serious harm has been done. This is not like in the world of mortals where officials set people up on purpose. Distinguished old sir, please raise your noble hand and forgive them. 'Even the planets do not orbit in perfect circles, much less are ghosts and spirits infallible.'" In the eyes of the God of Death, the deciding factor was whether there was any ulterior motive or not.

Recently, I heard a new story. A wealthy surgeon established a company and invited his middle school classmate to serve as the chairman of the board. The position was a sinecure and he could claim fifty thousand RMB per annum without ever having to go into the office. That man had been laid off and was on his uppers, beset with every kind of worry. This offer came as timely rain. He thought that the iron tree was about to break into blossom and his luck would alter on reaching

他一个良医,其他都是刽子手。"但几年之后公司违法经营被绳之以法,董事长是首犯,及时雨变成了六月雪,他是欲哭无泪,毕竟几年的钱是自己亲手拿了的。同学还是同学,医生还是医生,只是他成了囚犯。

把这件事说给平凹主编,顺茬说到心中贼。他说以前去一个村子,见过一个废置的土地庙,门前的对联字迹已模糊了,但字还能认全,写的是:"这一街许多笑话,我二老全不做声。"

middle age. With profound gratitude he accepted the certificate of appointment. Henceforth, wherever he went, he would gush panegyrics of praise about his old classmate, claiming that he was the only competent surgeon in the whole city and the rest were just butchers. Several years later, the company faced accusations of business malpractice. As chairman of the board he was fingered as the prime suspect. The timely rain had become June snow. He wanted to weep, but there were no tears in his eyes. After all, for years he had been receiving a stipend from that organisation. His classmate was still his classmate and the surgeon was still a surgeon. Only now, he faced incarceration.

I repeated this story to Jia Pingwa and at the same time raised the topic of thieves in the heart. He replied that he had once been to a village where he saw a derelict temple dedicated to the God of Earth. The couplet on its front gate had almost been worn away, but the letters were still legible in outline. It read, "This one street is rife with quips. We two seniors hold our lips."

代价与成本

一个国家的进步,是有代价和成本的。

为了不改变,最好的办法就是不交往,把社会封闭起来。清朝覆灭之前,我们一直都是这么干的,外国的使团,基本上都被视为为效忠而来。交往是彼此看重,但交往的核心价值,是建立自我更新系统,使自身不断强化。清朝因封闭而终结,但接下来开始的"交往",实在是让中国人脸面无光。二十世纪,是大中华漫漫历史中,唯一一个失去过自信力的一百年,洋车、洋火、洋蜡、洋油,东洋与西洋的东西,几乎渗入所有角落。乃至今天,从开发商新建楼盘的洋名字,到大学课堂上的洋学说,风

Price and Cost

There is a price and a cost with regard to a country's progress.

The best way to resist change is to relinquish communication and seal off a society from the outside world. The Chinese behaved like this before the fall of the Qing Dynasty. All of the foreign envoys were considered to have come to China to demonstrate their fealty. Communication involves mutual respect, though the core value of communication is to construct a system of self-renewal and to cultivate one's strength. The Qing Dynasty perished because of its isolationism. The exchanges which occurred subsequently caused the Chinese people to lose face. The twentieth century was the only one in the history of China in which she was forced to relinquish her confident front. Whether they came from the East or the West all those goods originating from abroad—foreign vehicles,

中国的风气

势正足。国家交往的危险，在于让本民族的遗传信息丢失了，像基因变异的植物，为改良而变种。确实，"洋为中用"带来了巨大变化，有经济的繁荣，也有文化的发展，正因为这种巨变，强化中国传统元素才显得更为迫切。一个国家的大学，特别是人文学科领域，自身元素不占上风，是让后辈人不幸的大事。

1792年9月26日，三艘大船组成七百人的英国使团，从朴茨茅斯港出发，目的地是中国，团长叫马戛尔尼勋爵。1793年9月14日，在承德避暑山庄，乾隆皇帝在"纸灯笼照耀着天子帷幄"

foreign matches, foreign candles and foreign paraffin—plugged almost every crevice in Chinese society. Even to this day, there is a predilection for foreign articles, in the names of newly-built projects by commercial construction companies or the theories taught in university classes. The pitfall in bilateral exchanges lies in the possibility that all national genetic information can be lost. It is a little like employing genetically modified technology to alter the seed of a plant. Indeed "making foreign things serve China" did deliver great changes to us, including economic prosperity and cultural development. On account of this profound development, there is an ever-pressing need to fortify traditional Chinese elements. The universities within a country, especially in the field of the humanities, feel that if one's own traditional elements cannot be made to hold sway, then the outcome will be lamentable for future generations.

On 26th September 1792, three large ships carrying seven hundred British envoys embarked from Portsmouth. Their destination was China. The leader of the delegation was Lord MacCartney. On 14th September 1793, the Emperor Qianlong greeted the visitors in "the curtained chamber illuminated

中国的风气

里，接见了使团的代表。其中给马戛尔尼提斗篷和下摆的是一位十二岁的男孩，叫托马斯·斯当东，就是这个小男孩，长大以后直接引发了两个国家的战争。他天资聪颖，在船上向担任翻译的教士学习汉语，乾隆因为他的"流利汉语"龙颜大悦，"解下挂在腰间的黄色丝织荷包，破例将它赐给孩子"。随庞大使团一起来到中国的，还有新发明的蒸汽机、棉纺机、织布机和热气球。乾隆的回答是天朝什么都不缺。他给英王的回赠是一件玉雕权杖，给马戛尔尼的是玉石节杖。

二十四年之后，1816年8月28日，英国第二个使团抵达北京，由阿美士德勋爵领衔，副职是已经三十六岁的托马斯·斯当东，此时他已在广州生活了多年，是英国东印度公司驻广州的商务

by paper lanterns" in the Chengde Summer Mountain Resort. The twelve-year-old boy who lifted the cloak and the lower hem of MacCartney's outfit was named Thomas Staunton and it was he who was to trigger war between the two nations as an adult. He was a prodigy, who learned the Chinese language from the missionary interpreter on the voyage over. Qianlong's dragon face lit up upon hearing his "fluent Chinese". He "unfastened the yellow silken pouch from his waistband and in an unprecedented gesture bestowed it upon the boy". Together with the huge delegation, the newly-invented steam engine, mechanised spinning frame and loom, as well as the hot air balloon, came to China. The Emperor Qianlong's reaction was that his Celestial Court was in want of nothing. In return he presented a carved jade mace intended for the King of England and a jade wand for MacCartney.

Twenty-four years later, on 28th August 1816, the second British delegation arrived in Beijing. The head of the delegation was Lord Amherst, with the now thirty-six-year-old Thomas Staunton as his deputy. Staunton had been residing in Guangdong for many years, where he acted as a

代表。但嘉庆皇帝没有接见他们,并且下令驱逐了使团。官方记录是,"中国为天下共主,岂有如此侮慢倨傲,甘心忍受之理。是以降旨逐其使团回国,不治重罪"。据坊间说法,原因有两个,一是特使不接受三拜九叩的觐见礼仪,二是斯当东的身份是商人,皇帝不能屈尊见商人。

又过了二十四年。1840年4月7日,六十岁的托马斯·斯当东在英国下议院"慷慨陈词":"我们进行鸦片贸易,是否违反了国际法呢?没有。……清廷有权强化司法措施以制止鸦片贸易。但迄今为止对外国人最重的处罚是禁止经商或驱逐出境。现在它能粗暴地判处他们死刑吗?……如果我们在中

representative of the British East India Company. However, the Emperor Jiaqing refused to meet them and had the party driven away. The official record states, "China is the master of all under heaven. It cannot tolerate such proud and supercilious behaviour. I ordered that they should retreat with haste, and they will not be punished for their heinous incursion." Popular retellings of the story proffer two explanations for this. One is that that British envoy declined to kneel down three times and kowtow nine times upon being received by the Emperor. The other is that Staunton was known to be a merchant. An Emperor could not condescend to meet an individual of his stripe.

Another twenty-four years passed by. On 7th April 1840, the almost sixty-year-old Thomas Staunton declared in the British House of Commons "with vehemence and excitement" that, "We are now engaged in the opium trade. Does this violate the international law? No... The Qing Government has the right to enforce its laws and prohibit the trade in opium. But up until now the most severe punishment that can be meted out on foreigners is to ban them from trading or have them expelled

国不受人尊敬，那么在印度我们也会很快不受人尊敬，并且逐渐地在全世界都会如此！尽管令人遗憾，但我还是认为这场战争是正义的，而且也是必要的。"一百八十多年前，英国人就是这么理解那场战争的。

1840年6月，一支由四十余艘战舰，四千多名士兵组成的舰队，经过孟加拉抵达广州海面。中国人丧失颜面的近代史生活，就此被强行拉开了序幕。

from the country. Right now are they able to rudely sentence them to execution? ... If we are not respected in China, then soon we will not be respected in India. The whole world would then follow suit. Even though it is a pity, I still maintain that this war is just and necessary." Over one hundred and eighty years ago, this was how British people believed that war was.

In June 1840, a fleet made up of over forty ships, carrying over four thousand soldiers docked at Guangdong, having passed through Bangladesh. From then on, the Chinese people were compelled to begin their lives without any face to lose.

立场与观念

用吹蜡烛的方式去吹灭一盏电灯是荒唐的,荒谬之处不是使用的方法,问题出在观念上。拉登是个危险人物,他的存在对人类来说就是潜在的威胁,但在基地组织内部,他是个受尊重的领导者,其中巨大的差异是因为所处的立场不同。

先说立场。

看一个喝水的杯子,角度不重要,杯子规模太小,可以一眼看穿。看一个独立的房子,角度的重要性就显示出来了。从前边看和从后边看是两回事,爬到房前的树上看又是另一回事。站在哪里看,那个位置,就是立场。

Positions and Ideas

It is ridiculous to try blowing out an electric light-bulb as one would a candle. The absurdity lies not in the method, but in the underlying idea. Bin Laden was a dangerous individual. His existence was a hidden threat for humanity, yet within Al-Qaeda he was held as a respectable leader. The great difference is that we find ourselves in different positions.

First, let us talk about positions.

Looking at a drinking cup, the angle is not significant. The size of the cup may be observed in one glance. Looking at an independent house, the angles are very significant. Looking at it from the front or from the back are two different matters. If one climbs the tree at the front of the house to take a look, that is another story too. The place where one chooses to stand when taking a look represents one's position.

中国的风气

看山和看河是不同的。山是静的，但四季有变化。河是每一刻都流动着，但四季变化不大。北方的河冬季要结冰，但这只是表面现象。看山，在山脚看和在山顶看不一样。住在山里的人和山外的游客对山的态度也不一样。鱼是水里的游客，却是河的家人，对河的态度与岸上人家不一样。大的河流，横看和竖看不一样，顺流看和上溯逆流看更不一样。子在"川上曰"的，虽然只是一句话，却沉淀着历史的高远和苍凉。

再说观念。

观念是活的，是随时事变化的。僵死的叫概念。观念是先进着好，掉在队

Looking at mountains is different from looking at rivers. Mountains are stationary, changing only with the seasons. Rivers are in perpetual motion. There are only slight changes in them through the seasons. The rivers in the north freeze during the winter, but this is only a surface phenomenon. Looking at mountains, there are differences between observing from the summit and observing from the base. Mountaineers and travellers from afar also have different attitudes towards mountains. Fish are the travellers in the water, but they are the kinsmen of the river. Their attitude towards the river is different from that of the people on the riverbank. Great rivers are different when observed from a horizontal or a vertical angle. They are more different still when seen from their downstream and their backflow. What Confucius commented on the riverbank is just a common saying, but it enshrined the loftiness and barrenness of the accumulated sediments of history.

Next, let us talk about ideas.

Ideas are alive. They change according to current events. Dead ideas are called "conceptions". Advanced ideas are good

伍后边的叫落伍。在队伍前面的是引导着变，在后面的是跟着变，好听一点儿叫应变。

以前的土地，是人的立身之本。土地是判断一户人家，或一个人价值的基本参照物。大户人家、殷实人家、破落人家的区分，就是以土地为标准。将军大臣，皇上要赐土地，自己也仗势圈地。商贾做大买卖的，要在乡下置地。有土地的人叫地主，在别人土地上干活的叫农民，农民不是职业，是身份的代称。土地所属的不平均，是造成社会不稳定，乃至动乱的根本因素，"揭竿而起"的主要原因是农民没有了活路和出路。

农本思想和田园经济是以前的核心

ideas. Those ideas which fall behind the times are labelled as "outdated". Those who take the lead at the front are at the vanguard of change. Those at the back follow these changes, or to use a better word, they "respond" to them.

Before, the land was the fundamental element of the people's existence. Land was the basic frame of reference by which the values of a family or a people were judged. Distinctions between large families, rich families, and broken families were determined by the extent of their land ownership. Generals and ministers had lands granted to them by the Emperor. They used their power to obtain further land and to expand their circle of influence. Those who were great businessmen would buy land in the countryside. Those who had land were called "landlords". Those who worked on others' lands were called "peasants". Being a peasant was not a profession. Rather, it was the pronoun which formed that person's identity. The imbalance of land ownership was the basic factor which brought about social instability and turbulence. The main cause of the "rise in rebellion" was that farmers had no means by which to live.

In former times, the core values were formed around the

中国的风气

价值观。

有一副老对联，"一等人忠臣孝子，两件事读书耕田"，以前的中国人，无论贵贱，人生理想就是这两件事，读书和耕田。当朝重臣求隐，叫"告老还乡"。一个将军赫赫战功之后，要"解甲归田"。如今观念变了，部长或将军退休，国家给退休金，不给土地。如今，农民有了自己的土地，人均有份。如果一种东西是平分的，这种东西的内在魔力就会下降，直至消失。从大趋势上讲，今天的农民是职业了，农民一词的内涵发生着变化，只是这变化还有待于被清晰化，被认识。"新农村建设""小城镇建设"，以及农村户籍改革，是政府在应变。

agricultural thought and the farm economy.

There is an ancient couplet: "First class citizens—faithful ministers and filial sons./ Two major concerns—reading books and ploughing the lands." In former times, no matter whether they were noble or humble, the Chinese people had two aspects to their ideal for life. These were reading books and ploughing the fields. If a high-ranking minister retired to become a hermit, this was labelled as an instance of "retiring and returning to one's native place". A great general, after having achieved notable success, would "take off his arms and return to the land". Nowadays, ideas have changed. If a minister or a general retires, the country will reward them with a pension, but not land. These days, the farmers have their own land. Each of them possesses their own share. If something is shared evenly, the inner magic of that entity will decrease and eventually disappear. Commenting on the larger trend, the farmer of today is professionalized. The connotation of this word has changed. The changes are not yet seen clearly and fully understood. "The construction of the New Countryside", "the construction of the New Township" and the reform of the household registration

土地观念发生了变化,以前的诗或文章,写田园乐、炊烟情,是写"主旋律",是呈现那时的核心价值。游子一词是针对故土说的,游子思乡也是主旋律的一种。但今天的作家再这么写,就叫落伍,或叫不合时宜。

system in the countryside mean that the government is responding to changes.

The idea of the land has changed. In former times, poetry and prose described the joy of the land, the affection of the smoke rising from the kitchen, and the "principal melody", which represented the core values of that time. The word "wanderer" refers to one who has gone away from his native place. The wanderer's nostalgia is also a kind of "principal melody", but if writers today carry on writing like this, it is called "out of date" or "out of keeping with the times".

会 说 话

嘴是工具，主要用途是吃饭喝水说话。至于其他的功能，由个人喜好而定，比如吹箫、吹笛子、吹唢呐。

说话直来直去着好，拐弯抹角的人不招待见。但有些特殊的场合，也是不宜开门见山的，要讲究说话的艺术，要会说话。

说三位大臣与帝王说话的典故。

晏婴是齐国的上大夫，相当于宰相。齐国有人得罪了齐景公，被绑押到大殿。齐景公发天威，下令把这个人肢解了，并且说，谁敢上谏一起杀。晏婴挽起袖子，亲自主刀。他左手按着那个

Knowing How to Talk

The mouth is a tool. Its main functions are eating, drinking and talking. As for its other uses, that is down to personal interest. One may, for instance, blow the panpipes, play the flute, blast away on the *suona*.

It is better to speak frankly. Those who prevaricate never make themselves popular. Even so, on some choice occasions, coming to the point is not the optimal means. The art of speech warrants attention. Learning to talk is a must.

I want to recount three anecdotes concerning exchanges between kings and their ministers.

Yan Ying was a high official in the State of Qi. His position was on a par with that of a prime minister. One subject of that state caused offence to King Jing and found himself bound up in ropes and hauled before the great hall of the Court. King Jing wielded his celestial prestige, decreeing that this blackguard

中国的风气

人的脑袋，右手"霍霍霍"磨着刀，朗声询问景公："陛下，古代明王圣主肢解人，从哪里下刀？"景公闻言，立即说："纵之，罪在寡人。"

简雍是刘备的"从事中郎"，相当于外交部部长。这个人很有水平，深得刘备的偏爱。朝中议事的时候，"独擅一榻"，仅在诸葛亮之下。这一年蜀逢大旱，估计是为了节约用水，政府出台了禁止酿私酒的法令。官员执法时，抓了一批家里藏着酿酒工具的人，准备对这些人依法论罪。一天，刘备和简雍在大街上微服私访，见一男一女有说有笑地闲走着，简雍说："这两人要行淫事，应该逮起来。"刘备问："你怎么知道？"

be torn limb from limb. The King, moreover, bellowed that whoever dared speak in the condemned man's defence would likewise forfeit their life. Yan Ying rolled up his sleeves and drew his dagger. He placed his left hand on the prisoner's head and sharpened the blade—*huo, huo, huo*—with his right hand. He asked the King in a raised voice, "Your Majesty, when the just and sainted kings of ancient times wanted to dismember convicts, where did they dig the knife in first?" On hearing these words, King Jing answered, "Let him go, the fault is mine."

Jian Yong was the "Foreign Minister" under Liu Bei. He was a distinctly learned man, especially in the eyes of Liu. Whenever any business was discussed in the Royal Court, he would be seated in a designated position just to the side of Zhuge Liang. One year, a serious drought struck the State of Shu. The government issued a decree prohibiting the private distillation of liquor. Perhaps this was a water conservation method. In the process of enforcing the law, the officials apprehended a number of people secretly harbouring stills and other contraband equipment at home. They prepared to mete out the punishments stipulated for this crime. One day Liu Bei

中国的风气

简雍回答:"这两人都带着行淫的工具呢。"刘备大笑,立即下令释放了藏酿酒工具的人。

有时候不说话,就是会说话。汉武帝刘彻的奶妈有恃无恐,做了一些过分的事,武帝知道后很生气,要严办。奶妈为保住一条命,去找东方朔求救。东方朔给出的"救命稻草"是:"无论皇帝怎么训责你,都听着,不要辩解。皇帝着人拉你出去的时候,也不要说话,多回头看他几眼,有眼泪最好。"奶妈就是这么做的。人心是肉长的,养育之恩比天高,比海深,武帝心底最柔弱的那块肉被激活了。"帝凄然,即赦免罪。"

and Jian Yong happened to be walking about the streets, making an inspection in nondescript plain clothes. They caught sight of a man and a woman laughing and talking together at leisure. Jian Yong said, "This pair is going to commit an obscene act and should be arrested at once." Liu Bei probed, "How do you know?" Jian Yong replied, "These two have the tools to fit the purpose." Liu Bei burst into laughter and ordered that all those found with spirit-making paraphernalia be let free.

Sometimes silence is more potent than words. Liu Che's (The Emperor Wu of Han Dynasty) wet nurse was complacent about having the backing of her superiors. As such, she broke the law indiscriminately. The news of her actions ignited Wu's fury and he wanted to punish her to death. In a bid to save her life, the wet nurse went to Dongfang Shuo for help. The "straw of hope" Dongfang extended to her was that, "No matter how seriously the Emperor scolds you, just listen and do not be contrary. When the Emperor orders that you be sent down, you should hold your tongue. Just turn your head back and try to fix him in the face. So much the better if tears are welling up in your eyes." The wet nurse did as what she was instructed. The

中国的政治史有两条主线索，一条是皇帝线，一条是宰相线。皇帝是抛物线，因为我们的皇帝是家庭承包制，个人能力的差异起伏巨大。宰相是水平线，基本上都在高水准上运行。好皇帝身边有名相，窝囊废皇帝更离不开名相。皇帝一言九鼎，无所谓会不会说话。但宰相必须具备两个基本功：会办事，会说话，历史上因为不会说话掉脑袋的宰相和名医不可胜数。

嘴是工具，说话时是传声筒，吃饭时是饭桶，真正的后台老板是心，是脑

human heart is a thing of flesh. The gratitude felt for the one who suckled you must be higher than the skies and deeper than the oceans. That piece of tender flesh inside Wu's breast was touched. "The sadness was too much for the Emperor to bear. He granted her a reprieve."

The history of Chinese politics has two guiding threads. One is the thread belonging to Emperors. The other is that belonging to prime ministers. The imperial thread is an arc because he is part of a household contract system. The personal aptitude of monarchs varies immensely. The prime ministerial thread is linear. They all swim in the highest stream. Good emperors are served by capable ministers, and incompetent emperors find themselves at their mercy. The ruler's words are authoritative, so they set no store by the art of talking. Prime ministers, however, rely on two qualities—knowing how to run a tight ship and knowing how to talk. In history, countless ministers and eminent royal physicians lost their heads because they were in want of tact.

The mouth is a tool. It can be employed as a megaphone. In eating it is a bucket for food. Its true but covert bosses are

子。"说话要凭良心""乱讲话,没脑子",坊间这两句俗话指的就是这层意思。其实写文章也是说话,只是工具变了,把嘴换成了笔。我觉得会说五句话,差不多就是一流文章。这五句话是:说人话,说实话,说家常话,说中肯的话,说有个性有水平的话。

the heart and brain. "Speak with a clear conscience" and "loose talk is witless talk"—these two everyday sayings bear this out. Writing an article is in fact a form of speech, only that an alternative set of tools is taken up. The mouth is substituted for a pen. I believe that the following five expressions are all one needs to compose a top notch article: speak human words, speak true words, speak household words, speak sincere words, and speak words with personality and wisdom.

玉皇大帝住什么房子？

玉皇大帝住什么房子？

吴承恩在《西游记》里是按人间帝王的标准设计的，吴承恩是明朝嘉靖年间的贡生，最高职位做到县丞，县丞就是县令的助手，老百姓尊称"八品县丞"。如今的作家挂职锻炼，也多任县丞级。《聊斋志异》的捉笔人蒲松龄是清朝的贡生，他官至县学的"儒学训导"，相当于县党校副校长。职位是虚设，因而才有闲情逸致搜集那么多闲闻野趣。贡生还有一个别称，叫举人副榜。两位留驻青史的超一流作家学历都不算高，但写作的大思路比较接近，都是旁走一辙，异想天开。神仙鬼怪的行为方式，临摹着人间烟火的标准，佛也

What Kind of House Did the Jade Emperor Live in?

What kind of house did the Jade Emperor live in?

In *The Journey to the West* the author Wu Cheng'en designed the Jade Emperor's residence according to those inhabited by rulers in the real world. Wu was the *gongsheng* (senior licentiate) in the Jiajing era of the Ming Dynasty. The highest rank he attained was *xiancheng*, that is to say the assistant to the county head. He was addressed as "the eighth-rank assistant to the county head" respectfully by the people. Nowadays, when writers are sent down to experience life in the provinces they will usually serve in a similar post. Pu Songling, the author of *Strange Tales from the Liaozhai Studio*, worked as a *gongsheng* in the Qing Dynasty. The most senior position he held was the Director of a Confucian Academy, which is on a par with the deputy head of a Communist Party county school in modern times. The job was a paper one, so his mind

受贿，鬼也多情。

玉帝是天尊，在吴承恩的笔下享受的却是人间天子的住房待遇，该算屈尊。吴承恩级别低，当年没有机会亲眼去看皇帝住什么样的房子，因此玉帝的住处也多是虚写。天庭里君臣答对也是依着宫廷廷对的样子。这一套他比较熟悉，没吃过羊肉，但羊怎么走他是知道的。

was not burdened and he had the leisure to be able to gather anecdotes and amusing stories. An alternative name for the *gongsheng* was *juren fubang* (qualified scholar in waiting). These two superlative authors, whose names are carved into the historical record, did not have first-rate diplomas, but they shared a comparable manner of thinking and writing. Both of them chose the road less travelled and gave full tilt to their imagination. The ghosts and spirits in their works mimicked the behaviour and lives of ordinary mortal folk. Buddhas may accept a bribe or ghosts might be led astray by passion.

The Jade Emperor is the paramount god. In Wu Cheng'en's works, his dwelling place is modelled on those of monarchs in this world. This can be construed as something of an affront. Wu's official position was low, so he had no opportunity to witness the imperial palaces firsthand. Thus he had to rely on his whimsy to sketch a home for the Jade Emperor. The dialogue between the Emperor and his ministers in the Heavenly Court also imitates its terrestrial counterparts. He was rather familiar with this type of business. He never tasted mutton himself, but knew how sheep gamboled.

称玉帝也叫万岁,皇上的住处叫宫殿,这是硬性规定。但比皇上级别高的,就不方便再叫别的了,想象力高却不逾矩,这是我们国人的文统意识。遇到高的不知怎么办,遇到低的敢于放开手提拔。比如美国总统的住处,英文叫白房子,含着与民同乐的平等意思,但我们的翻译界却译为"白宫"。再比如,婴儿出生前的住处,叫子宫。每个人出生前都是享受帝王待遇的,这是我们国人的人生观,"天之大德曰生"。普通人家的孩子出生叫落草,因为普通人的大名叫草民。

Wu therefore addressed the Jade Emperor as the dear ruler who should "live ten thousand years" (*wansui*). The home of the Emperor was rendered as "the palace" (*gong*), yet in the order of things he could find no proper name for the residence of the immortals whose rank was supposedly higher than this leader of flesh and blood. Chinese people have a common comprehension of what literature should do. Namely, there is a habituation towards showing imagination whilst not transgressing boundaries. In the face of their superiors, they are at a loss. In the face of their inferiors, they act as they see fit. For example, in English the residence of the US president is known as the "White House". That carries the connotation of being on an equal footing with the public. Chinese translators favour the expression "White Palace" (*Baigong*). Another example is how in China before an infant is born the womb he inhabits is called the "kid's palace" (*zigong*). This means that in the prenatal stage, everyone is as privileged as an emperor. "The greatest concern of heaven is to foster new life." This is the Chinese view of life. When a child is born into an ordinary family, his or her birth is described as "tumbling into the grass" (*luocao*) because

中国的风气

旧小说在旧文学里是不入流的,上不了大席面。小说的名称以小字开头,不是自谦,不是小得如何如何的意思。叫小说是旧文学观。散文是立言,是树人,是文之正。小说是闲情逸致,是纯粹的业余写作。用流行过的那个词说,散文是大我,小说是小我。旧小说的基础是街巷掌故和乡野故事,写作形式受评书的直接影响,因此小说的结构形式以"回"分列,每一章结束的那句话是"且听下回分解",接下来新的一章又以"上回说到"开始。中国的旧小说在世界文学史里是最具听觉效果的,旧小说写家最大的虚荣是被一流的说书人选中。如今的新小说追求视觉效果,进电视,入电影院,一部小说被名导演选中,名头再重的作家也要偷着乐几回。时代变迁了,新旧小说已经完全是两回事,如今的小说是新文学里的正果,是

the majority of people belong to the grassroots (*caomin*).

In ancient times the novel did not belong to the mainstream in Chinese society. It was not worthy to be conferred on a grand occasion. The Chinese word for novel is "small talk" (*xiaoshuo*). The prefix "small" is employed not out of modesty or on account of the tiny scale of such a work. "Small talk" enshrines the old view of literature. To set down prose is to "expound one's ideas" (*liyan*) and to "establish an exemplar" (*shuren*). Hence, that mode was upheld as the apotheosis of literary endeavour. The novel can be counted as a diversion, the contrivance of a leisurely and carefree mood. It belongs absolutely to the preserve of writing for pleasure. To express this in fashionable parlance, prose is about "magnifying one's ego" (*dawo*) whereas the novel is about "masking one's ego" (*xiaowo*). The basic material for every novel composed in China is "tittle tattle from the streets and alleys". The style is directly influenced by the narrative form of the storytelling script. Consequently, novels are divided into chapters and at the end of each lies a statement encouraging readers to carry on if they want to know what will happen next. The ensuing

正宗。一个人写了几本散文，几本诗，分量上是比不过一本小说的。稍有一点点遗憾的，是小说这个名称，当兵打仗时叫二狗，如今做了上将军，名字也该换换了。

我们旧小说里有三种东西，让外国的读者不太好理解。一是传奇志异类的，仙女下凡或狐仙、蛇仙主动变幻成

chapter will start by expressly picking up where the action left off. More so than any other literature throughout the world, the tales found in ancient Chinese novels entered the repertoire of oral storytellers. The greatest vanity for a writer in the old days was to hear his works issuing from the mouths of such performers. In the present day, novels strive to arrest the eyes, the greatest aspiration being to spawn a TV or movie adaptation. If an author's work is selected by a director, no matter how renowned he is already the creator will be privately in raptures. Times have changed. Ancient novels and modern novels are completely different. The novel has now been installed as the apotheosis of literary endeavour. The scribbler of several chapbooks of prose or verse cannot be considered as the novelist's peer. The only regrettable matter is how the genre still bears the same nametag. A soldier on the frontline can be called a "scrapping dog" (*ergou*), though on being promoted as a general he must shed such labels.

There are three aspects of the Chinese novel which foreigners find hard to comprehend. The first is the inclusion of supernatural tales. Fairies, fox or snake spirits metamorphose

人形，目的是享受人世的美好生活。在外国的童话和传说里，则是由人变成动物，其中有一些是巫术导致的，但结局是良心和正义占了上风，真相大白后，还要变回去。我们的就不变了，除非犯了错误，或本事太大，引起了神鬼界的不满。鬼怪为摆脱阴暗的日子到人间还好理解一些，不好理解的是，鬼怪又出奇地美丽和善良，仙女思凡的细节更不好接受。在外国人的认识里，神就是神，在天堂大门的那一边，偶尔出来做些善事还可以，到这边来过日子是纯粹的中国制造。一位搞文学研究的外国人这么写："在中国小说里，大的神要设法管住小的神，尤其是漂亮的女神，不让她们嫁到人间。"

into human form. Their purpose is to revel in the beauty of our existence. In fairy tales and legends from abroad, it is typical that people are transformed into animals. Some of this magic results from sorcery. The resolution of the story marks a victory for justice and the noble conscience, with the changeling being restored to his or her former identity as soon as the truth is revealed. In China there is no reversion unless the character commits a mistake or overstretches their power. In either case, the spirits are exasperated and curtail the adventure as punishment. It is easy to understand why ghosts wish to escape their gloomy exile and migrate to the land of the living. What is more challenging to accept is how these entities are portrayed as being so elegant and magnanimous. Beyond that, how is one to believe that captivating fairy maidens might crave a mortal existence like ours? In foreigners' eyes, a deity is a deity. Paradise is their habitation, yet they may occasionally venture outside to perform some benevolent intervention. As far as having deities live in our midst is concerned, that is an invention "made in China". A foreign expert on literature wrote, "In the Chinese novel, senior deities always try to control

第二种是老实人形象。一个男人其貌不扬,本事稀松平常,日子过得也寒酸,最大的优点是老实本分。突然有一天,仙女或狐仙、蛇仙出现了,想尽一切方法,冲破层层阻隔终于嫁给了他。这种事被外国人读成是中国的说教智慧。他们知道吃不到葡萄说葡萄酸的故事,但不知道中国还有一个成语,叫望梅止渴。

第三种是旧小说叙述形式里的开头诗和结尾诗。一篇外国文章解读为:"小说开头的诗介绍故事梗概,这是出版商做的事。小说告一段落或结尾的诗是道德评点,但这可不是好的书评人乐于做的事。"另一篇文章说的好听一些,中国小说里开头和结尾的诗"似乎是叙

inferior deities, especially in preventing matrimony between delectable deities and mere mortals."

The second aspect is the figure of the incorrigibly honest man. This type of personage is plain in appearance, not precocious and ekes out a pitiful and poor life. His prime merit is his honest simplicity. Suddenly one day, a fairy or fox spirit or snake spirit comes along and tries every means and tramples over every barrier to win his hand in marriage. Foreigners regard this kind of trope as being like a sermon, enshrining Chinese wisdom. They know the tale of how when you cannot reach a bunch of grapes you insist they must be sour. On the other hand, they are unfamiliar with the Chinese proverb: "Curb your thirst by staring at the plum."

The third aspect is the poems which precede the narrative of a novel or act as a corollary. One article by a foreign critic reads, "The verse at the beginning of a novel lays out its bare outline. This is the embellishment by the publisher. The verse at the end is an ethical appraisal. A discerning reviewer would not pass comment on them." Another article by a foreigner has a nice ring to it, namely identifying these poems as "the escort

述的护舰队和卫兵"。

　　旧小说尽管有不少"陋习",但读着真过瘾、真文学,也真中国化。仅仅是读着文字,都是一种大享受。因为爱读这些"旧货",对评论这些"旧货"的文字也捎带着看一点儿。洋行家写的没什么意思,他们对中国文化的底子知道得太少。我们自己新行家写的也不太喜欢,新行家用的也多是"先锋"的洋理论,夹杂着半生不熟的译文体的学术单词,读起来不对味儿,感觉是用裁制西装的尺子比量唐装。现在不少工厂都在讲"本土化"的话题,贴牌生产的产品在大幅减少,好像文学研究界这边动静不太大。

　　最近省上一位退下来的重要领导,要我推荐几本小说,我买了一套"禁毁小说"送给他,厚厚的十大本,是几十

and guard of the narrative".

Although ancient novels contain many effete habits, they arouse satisfaction and give the impression of being authentically literary and inimitably Chinese. A great pleasure can be derived from perusing the letters on the page. Since I love to read these "old things", I sample the remarks others have made about them. Foreigners tend not to pass penetrating judgements owing to the paucity of their background knowledge. Likewise, I have disdain for the essays by so-called "new experts" in China. In the main these flaunt avant-garde theories appropriated from the West. Their articles are laced with half-baked jargon in translation, which are insipid on the palette. It is akin to using an imported measuring tape to recreate uniforms from the Tang Dynasty. At present, so many factories emphasise localisation and far fewer products have foreign labels superimposed on them. In literature, there is apparently no comparable trend.

Lately, a retired provincial senior cadre asked me to recommend a few novels and so I purchased a set of "banned publications" for him. This was a hefty, ten-volume collection

中国的风气

部明清小说的合集。一周过后,他告诉我:"好呀,好呀,真是好。"他说现在的有些小说虚假,但胆子大,不熟悉的都敢写,列举了几本"著名的反腐小说"的名目。他说的有趣:"小说情节与现实相比有些失真,细节不真实,开会不是那么开会。"我告诉这位领导:"这怪不得作家,作家挂职多数才是副县级,对政治生态的了解也就有限了。"

吴承恩真是了不起,对不熟悉的生活,他不敢把笔落得太细致。

consisting of dozens of Ming and Qing Dynasty novels. One week later, he told me, "They're good, really good." To his mind, some of the novelists of today are pretentious yet bold. They write about what they don't know. He reeled off several famous titles dealing with cracking down on corruption. His remarks were amusing, "The plots are a bit distorted compared to reality. The details are pure fiction. Meetings are not conducted in that way." I responded, "The authors themselves are not to blame. When they were sent to work in the provinces, most of them only served as the assistants to the county head. Therefore, their understanding towards political ecology is limited."

Wu Cheng'en is awesome. Matters unfamiliar to him were never gone into with too much precision.

写散文要说人话

散文是说话。说人话，说实话，说中肯的话。

说人话。不要说神话，除非你是老天爷。不要说鬼话，除非你是无常。也不要说官话，就是个官，也要去掉官气，官气在官场流通，在文章里要清除。也不要说梦话，文章千古事，要清醒着写文章。说正常人的话，说健康人的话，说实话。实有结实、果实、现实等内涵。结实是不虚枉，有实质内容。果实是结果，好文章里有思考，还有思想。农民种庄稼，不仅仅看长势喜人，最终还要看收成。文学写作要关注现实也要切合现实，切合现实不是在鼓与呼那个层面，而是既要写出时代气息，还

To Write a Prose is To Say Human Words

Prose is a form of speech. One can only speak in human language, using words which are truthful and meant sincerely.

To speak in human language means not to speak in the language of the gods, unless you are a heavenly being. Do not utter the language of ghosts unless you are the grim reaper. What is more, do not adopt the tone of an official. Even if you are in fact an official, you should not put on airs. The air of an official can be vented in the realms of officialdom, but when it comes to prose writing, such haughtiness ought to be weeded out. Avoid the language of dreams as well. Writing is the distillation of thousands of years of praxis. Write articles when you are sober-minded, and express yourself in the manner of a normal and healthy person. Use words which are truthful. Truthful words are solid, fecund and close to reality. Solidity implies the opposite of emptiness and means to carry authentic

中国的风气

要深入把握社会特征和规律，以及趋势。什么是社会趋势呢？比如"三十年河东，三十年河西"，这是民谚，是大实话。以二十世纪一百年做观照，1919到1949是三十年，1949到1979是三十年，这期间的两个三十年之变均是天翻地覆式的。

真话也是实话，是落在实处的话。真话是不穿漂亮衣裳的，不乔装打扮，没有扮相。真话可能不中听，甚至刺耳，可能还讨人嫌。但真话的难得之处在于对事物的认知上有突破和新发现。

content. Fecundity denotes having a positive outcome. Good articles convey good reasoning and good thoughts. When a farmer tends his crops, he is concerned with both the daily growth and the ultimate harvest. Literary writing should also focus on reality and, in fact, cling to it. Clinging to reality does not infer clapping one's palms and declaiming a message loudly. It should not only register the pulse of the age, but also grasp the characteristics, rhythm and trends therein. What then are social trends? For instance, there is a folk proverb, "Thirty years on the east bank of the river, and thirty years on the west." This sentence rings quite true. Let us take the last century as a point of reference. From 1919 to 1949 thirty years elapsed and from 1949 to 1979 another thirty years elapsed. During these two phases of three decades, the changes were so acute that the heavens and the earth seemed to have shifted places.

True words are also solid words which are effective and practical. True words wear no showy clothes, nor do they dress up or have the appearance of an actor. True words may not always sound good. They might even grate on one's ears. True words could raise the hackles of people. They are rare because

实话可以实说，也可以打比方说，遇到脾气不好又强势的听者，还可以绕弯子说，但无论怎么说，说话者的心态要平和。跳着脚说，挥舞着拳头说，精神抖擞着说，呼哧带喘着说，义愤填膺怒发冲冠着说，是说话时表情丰富。如果觉着解气过瘾，可以这么既歌之又舞之，但不宜养成这么说话的习惯，太劳碌身体。

真话不在高处，真话是寻常的话，是普通话。如果一个时期里，说真话被当成高风亮节，被视为稀罕物，这个时期就是悲哀的，是社会的悲哀。检测社会是否悲哀的方法也简单，翻翻报纸，看看电视，听听广播，瞅瞅杂志，心里

they are innovative and shed a fresh understanding of the world.

Solid words can be stated in a solid manner. They can, moreover, make use of analogy and example. When ill-tempered and haughty listeners are present, solid words may provide a means of beating around the bush. However, no matter how one uses them, the speaker should maintain a calm mind. Speaking in high spirits, with one's ankles springing and fists waving, or gasping for breath, or with hair on end and flushed with anger—these are the battery of rich emotions an orator can deploy. If one simply speaks for the sake of self-satisfaction and to vent personal discontent, speech becomes like a song and dance routine. On balance, it is not healthy to cultivate such a habit. The body is overly-taxed by this.

True words are not lofty but ordinary. If in a particular era, telling the truth is regarded as a rare practice or as a sign of noble character, then that period and society must be benighted. By scanning the newspapers, watching television broadcasts, listening to the radio and skimming through magazines, it is very easy to gauge whether a society is benighted and sad or

就有个大概了。建设文明社会,民风朴素重要,文风实实在在同样重要。社会文明,不一定天天跟过节似的,到处莺歌燕舞,而是惠风和畅,民心踏实安定。

说中肯的话,是有原则,守边界。生活里,说大话的人是不招待见的。大话不是空话,是一望无际,没着落。文章是写给人看的,话是说给人听的,因此要中肯,要让人接受。中肯的话也是家常话,"老僧只说家常话",修行中的小和尚才言不离经,手不释卷的。"逢人只说三分话,未可全抛一片心",这样的话是说给大街上的陌生人的,这不是家常话,是客气话。

写散文,要爱惜语言,神枪手是心疼手中武器的。我们的古汉语博大精

not. In order to build a civilised society, a basic and sincere etiquette must be cultivated in much the same way as these qualities are nurtured in writing. Having a civilised society does not mean that every day is like a festival and that swallows and warblers cavort and twitter all over the place. Rather the people are caressed by a smooth and gentle breeze and can cherish a sense of safety and inner calm.

Speaking sincere words means to have principles and boundaries. In life, people dislike those who talk big. Big talk is not empty talk, but endless ranting without limits. Articles are written for people to read; words are spoken for people to hear. Thus, the content must be sincere and acceptable. Sincere words are household words. "The aged monk only speaks household words", while novices always have the sutras in their hands and on their lips. "Never show your whole heart, only share thirty percent of what is in your mind." This refers to words spoken to strangers on the street. They are exchanged out of politeness and are not household words per se.

In writing a piece of prose, one must cherish the vocabulary. A marksman cherishes the weapon in his hands.

深，老到沉实。现代汉语才走过百年的道路，一百年，对人来说是高寿，但对十几亿人使用的一门语言，还年轻着，因为年轻，我们更该爱惜。

回首现代汉语的百年道路，有两个基本点值得检讨。一是自卑心理，白话文被倡导的时候，向国外学习得多，向古汉语学习得少，至今这种心理阴影仍在，一些没有消化妥当的翻译词、译文句仍然显著。今天强调建立文化自信，有太多的基本东西需要被认识到。二是文风上受当时二十世纪六七十年代风潮的影响，语言风格过于浮华，外包装太多，不实在，而且情绪化，反理性。狂轰滥炸式的，太不爱惜语言。现代的文学是用现代汉语做基础材料的，做大建筑，基础材料仅仅过关不行，还要过硬。

To Write a Prose is To Say Human Words

The ancient Chinese language is broad and profound, elegant and substantial. Modern Chinese only stretches back one hundred years. For a man, living a century represents great longevity. For a language shared by billions of people, it is still juvenile. On account of this juvenility, it requires more solicitude.

Tracing back the developmental journey of modern Chinese, we need to be critical on two basic points. One concerns an inferiority complex. When the use of vernacular Chinese was advocated, we tried to learn more from abroad, but in fact absorbed less from our own ancient heritage. Even nowadays, this casts a shadow over our psychology. Some improper and half-digested loanwords remain popular. These days, when we emphasise the building of cultural confidence, there are too many basic elements which need to be reexamined. The other thing is that literary style bears the influence of the trend of the 1960s and 1970s. The language is superficial with too much surface ornament and too little core. It is emotional, even irrational. In this bombardment of language, the vocabulary is not cherished in the least. The

今天的散文写作，文学标准也是不太清晰的。在散文这个概念之外，还有杂文、随笔、小品文等名目。小说以长篇、中篇、短篇区分，诗歌以抒情、叙事、哲理等区分，但散文内涵和外延的界定比较模糊，有待研究界做出理论的梳理与认知。还有一个事实，在文学研究界，如果把西方文论的东西拿掉，所剩的东西不太多。当代文学研究，有点儿类似当下的汽车制造业，整条生产线都是进口的，没有实现"中国制造"。也就是说，我们目前还没有建立起中国人思维基础上的当代文学评价体系。不仅文学研究界，在不少领域，我们都欠缺自己的标准。中国的经济总量在世界名列前茅，这是改革开放以来取得的巨

modern Chinese language is the basic material for modern Chinese literature. In constructing a grand building, the basic materials should not only be merely adequate, but of premium quality.

The literary criteria for prose writing in the present day are not so clear. Beyond the overall concept of prose, there is the essay, the literary note and the sketch. As for fiction, there is the novel, the novella and the short story. For poetry, there are lyric, narrative and philosophical divisions. As far as the connotations and denotations of prose are concerned, its definitions are confusing. We are waiting for a theoretical combing and cognition to be initiated in this research field. Another fact must be taken into account. Namely, if we sweep away all western theories from the study of literature, very little is left behind. The status quo of contemporary literary studies is somewhat like that of the automobile industry. The complete assembly line is imported. We do not achieve the target of being "made in China". That is to say, we have yet to establish a contemporary system for literary evaluation based upon Chinese modes of thinking. Not only in the field of literary

中国的风气

大成就，但这个排名标准是西方的。经济、教育、医疗、环保，以及工业和农业的一些具体指标，所使用的标准，"国产化"程度不太高。

建设强大国家，应该强大在根子上，我们已经到了建立中国人标准的时候了，包括中国人的文学标准。

studies, but in numerous others do we lack our own self-defined benchmarks. China's aggregate economy has ploughed on ahead. This sprawling achievement has been made since we opened up to the outside world. Still, the criteria for this ranking were determined according to western standards. For every index and criterion relating to economics, education, medicine, environmental protection, industry and agriculture, we lack a domestic standard.

In building a great nation, we should insist on greatness from the very root. It is high time for us to establish Chinese criteria. This is true of Chinese literature too.

言者无罪：
中国早期的民意调查

周代的采诗官，是中国最早的职业民调人员。

春天到了，农耕在望，百废待兴，又一个轮回的忙忙碌碌即将启动。在这个节骨眼上，各诸侯国的采诗官们开始了他们的工作，这些人"衣官衣"，手持木铎，铎是古代政府发布号令的响器，分为两种，"以木为舌则曰木铎，以金为舌则曰金铎"。宣布政令以木铎，发布军令以金铎，"文事奋木铎，武事奋金铎"。深入民间，沿途征集抒写民情民愿的诗，之后由专门的音律官员整理，配上音乐，由诗而歌，唱给周天子，中国人称诗为"诗歌"由此开始。唱给周天子的诗有一个标准，"采诗，

Blame Not the Speaker:
The Early Opinion Poll in China

The poetry collectors in the Zhou Dynasty were surely the earliest opinion pollsters in China.

When spring came around, the planting season was nigh and all was waiting expectantly to be reinvigorated. Another cycle of frenzied activity was about to begin. In this crucial moment, the officials tasked with gathering poetry in each kingdom commenced their work. These people wore "official garbs" and carried a wooden clapper in one hand. In ancient times the clapper was the instrument used to sound official orders. It was divided into two categories: "The type crafted from wood and the type cast in metal." The former was reserved for issuing civil orders and the latter for military commands. Those public servants went to the countryside and mingled among the populace, collecting poetry which described the desires and feelings of ordinary people. Once gathered together,

中国的风气

采取怨刺之诗也",怨刺诗,即以民怨、民伤、刺政为主要内容。这样的诗中,可能有过头的话,却是真实的心底声音,周代的政治高层据此洞察民心动向。国家如没有重大的政德和军功事件发生,泛泛的歌功颂德作品被视为"下作",不在征集采撷之列。

古代的中国人,判断一件事情的是非曲直,首先考察"初心",即做事情的动机。无端或没来由的恭维奉承他人,被认为是动机不纯。孔子编选《诗

the collation process would be undertaken by personnel from the academy of music. They would set the verses to musical scores and then send them to the capital city to be sung before the King of Zhou. That is when the Chinese started to address poetry as "verse and song" (*shige*). The poetry sung before the King of Zhou had to meet certain criteria. "The collected poetry must consist of complaints and satires." The principal content dealt with the sorrows and complaints of the people, including satire directing at the government. Some of the statements made therein might be hyperbolic, yet each spoke with a voice arising from the bottom of a person's heart. The ruling class of the Zhou Dynasty possessed insight into the motivations of the ordinary people. If the government achieved nothing significant in either the civil or military spheres, those "potboilers" which sang the praises of the administration would not be included in the collection.

In ancient times the Chinese people judged right and wrong in the first instance according to "original aspiration", namely the motives behind a person's actions. Unreasonable and illogical flattery were regarded as a symptom of an

经》的时候，在艺术标准之外，还有一个道德人心标准，"诗三百，一言以蔽之，思无邪"，《诗经》三百零五首诗，用一句话概括，写作的初心都在人间正道上，不旁逸邪出，不走小道，也不抄近路。这也是周代初年实行的"采诗制度"的基本原则。

周代的政府，重视倾听民间的真实声音，不禁言，这是特别了不起的。

采诗，后人衍为采风，取义《诗经》中的"国风"，指意更加具体明确：关注民情，采集人间疾苦。

ulterior motive. When Confucius compiled *The Book of Songs*, apart from the artistic standard, he also had a further moral criterion. "In *The Book of Songs*, there are three hundred pieces, but the design of them all may be embraced in one sentence — 'Having no depraved thoughts.'" The three hundred and five poems in the volume can be summarised with a single sentence: "The original aspiration." Composing poetry was always stuck to the great road of righteousness, never aiming to be vicious or deceptive, never resorting to narrow paths or relying upon shortcuts. These are the basic principles of the "poetry collecting system" adopted in the early days of the Zhou Dynasty.

The government of the Zhou Dynasty paid attention to the voice of the grassroots. It did not censor opinions. This was really something great.

Later on, poetry collecting veered towards gathering samples of folklore. Actually, this was a deviation from the "ballads" which constitute *The Book of Songs*. The motivations for this activity had become more concrete and clear, namely showing concern for the lives of ordinary people and preserving

《汉书·食货志》对采风制度的记载:"孟春三月,群居者将散,行人振木铎徇于路以采诗,献之大师,比其音律,以闻于天子,故曰王者不窥牖户而知天下。"周代的历法,以冬至所在月份为一年的岁首正月,即今天的农历十一月。孟春三月,是今天历法的农历正月。冬天的闲聚生活即将结束,人们要各自忙碌去了。采诗官采风以后献给音律官员,使周天子不用出宫廷就悉知天下事态。

their sorrows.

In *The Book of Han: Records of Livelihood*, there is an account of the system for collecting folklore: "In the first month of spring, the people who had gathered together were about to scatter. The officials who collected poetry travelled along the road with a wooden clapper. They donated what they had gathered to the officials at the academy of music, who in turn composed accompaniments and offered up the songs for the king's appreciation. Hence the king came to know what was going on under the heavens without having to poke his nose into every household." In the calendar of the Zhou Dynasty the first month of the year began with the solstice, which in the present day falls in November. The first month of the spring in the calendar of that time of the year was what is now the first month of the entire year. The leisurely life of winter was about to end and the people were readying themselves for the activities of spring. The poetry collectors presented what they had collected to the officials in charge of music. Therefore, the monarch of Zhou learned what was happening outside without having to leave his palace.

采诗官由年长者担任，中央及地方均有此职位，《春秋公羊传注疏》记载："男年六十，女年五十无子者，官衣食之，使之民间求诗，乡移於邑，邑移於国，国以闻於天子。"官衣，着政府官员制服。食之，享受官员待遇，但不是正式官员，用今天的话讲，是比照公务员待遇。采诗官由无子者担任，是防范民调人员的挟私之心。古人重男轻女，有女儿也视为无子。

The poetry collecting officials were usually senior in age. They occupied positions both in the central and the local governments. *Notes on Biography of Gongyang in Spring and Autumn* states, "When a man reaches the age of sixty, or a woman fifty, and is still childless, the government provides them with official clothing and state rations of food. They are to venture into the countryside to collect poetry, transferring what they gleaned to the province in question. Thereafter the province would convey that data to the capital, so that it eventually reaches the ears of the king." The expression "official clothing" denotes that they were allowed to wear the garments set aside for government officials. "State rations" signifies that although they were not bona fide officials they could nevertheless enjoy their victuals. In the parlance of the present day, they were the "civil servants under the state". The reason why childless individuals were singled out for this duty was to guard against these opinion pollsters becoming selfish-minded. In ancient China, sons were valued and daughters disdained. Those who had daughters but no sons were classed as "childless" as well.

中国的风气

大时代是由大人物开创的,并由一系列不平凡的制度构成的。在国家制度上有突破,有建立,是大时代的标识。孔子终生念念不忘的"克己复礼",礼就是指规矩和制度,旨在重返西周的制度时代。

孟子在《离娄》中对采诗制度的兴衰做了总结,"王者之迹熄而诗亡,诗亡然后《春秋》作"。诸侯国(地方势力)做大做强之后,周天子对国家局面失去控制(指东周之后),支流漫过主流,采诗制度就终结了,之后《春秋》问世。

孔子从三千多首采诗作品中,十中取一,精选出一部《诗经》,初名为

A great era is forged by great characters. It comprises a series of extraordinary systems. The hallmark of a great era is that breakthroughs and bold achievements are made in the national system. What Confucius bore in mind throughout his life was how one should "subdue one's self and return to propriety". "Propriety" here refers to systems and rules and regulations, so he was encouraging a return to the system at work in the Western Zhou Dynasty.

In his work *Li Lou*, Mencius summarised the rise and fall of poetry collecting system. He wrote, "The traces of sovereign rule were extinguished, and the royal odes ceased to be made. When those odes ceased to be made, then the *Spring and Autumn Annals* was produced." As the power of local chiefs increased, the King of Zhou lost his authority over the country at large (this refers to the time after the Eastern Zhou). With the branches becoming stronger than the trunk, the poetry collecting system drew to an end. After this time, the *Spring and Autumn Annals* appeared.

Confucius selected one-tenth of the more than three thousand poems collected hitherto and compiled *The Classic of*

《诗》，汉代之后称《诗经》。思想家的孔子，做了一回编辑家，应该理解为是圣人对采诗制度的致敬和缅怀。司马迁在《史记》中对此也做了记载："古者诗三千余篇，及至孔子，去其重，取可施于礼义……三百五篇孔子皆弦歌之，以求合韶、武、雅、颂之音，礼乐自此可得而述。"

《诗经》在秦始皇时期，经历过"焚书"浩劫，《焚书令》规定："天下敢有藏《诗》《书》、百家语者，悉诣守、尉杂烧之。有敢有偶语《诗》《书》者，弃市。"

到了汉代，《诗经》成为治世之书，

Poetry, which after the Han Dynasty became known as *The Book of Songs*. As a thinker, Confucius at this time turned his hand to being an editor. This may be interpreted as the sage's respect for and yearning after the former system for collecting poetry. In *Records of the Grand Historian*, Sima Qian wrote, "There were more than three thousand ancient songs, but Confucius rejected those which were repetitious and retained those which had moral value... Confucius chose three hundred and five songs in all, and he set these to music and sang, fitting them to the music of Emperor Shun and King Wu, odes and hymns. After that the old rites and music became widely known."

During the reign of the First Emperor of Qin, *The Book of Songs* fell victim to the "book burning" campaign. The royal decree stated, "Whoever under the heavens, is found to have retained editions of *The Book of Songs* and *The Classic of History* or selections from the One Hundred Schools of Thought should have these works confiscated and incinerated. If anybody dares to discuss these works in private, they should be beheaded in public."

During the Han Dynasty, *The Book of Songs* was transformed

位列"五经"之首,并且开创了一个官员选拔制度——察举制,饱读"五经"的人才可以做官,这个制度到后来完善为科举制。秦始皇焚书,《诗经》和《尚书》列为首禁之书,是禁思想。而汉代奉立"五经",使之作为治国之书,也在于其中的思想之重,这是汉代之所以成为大时代的一个重要根基所在。

唐代的白居易作《采诗官》对采诗制度曾发出遥远的感慨:

采诗官,
采诗听歌导人言。
言者无罪闻者诫,

into a guide for social governance and listed as the first among the Five Classics. Moreover, it inspired the creation of a new system for selecting officials (involving inspection and recommendation). Those who were well-versed in the Five Classics were entitled to be selected as officials. Later on, this system gradually evolved into the imperial examination. When the First Emperor of Qin decreed that books should be burned, *The Book of Songs* and *The Classic of History* were the first to be outlawed. This was in an effort to circumscribe freedom of thought. Then, in the Han Dynasty the Five Classics were adopted as the template for state governance, which was another instance of the authorities acknowledging the potency of free thought. This was the fundamental reason why the Han Dynasty became a golden age in Chinese history.

In the Tang Dynasty Bai Juyi once breathed a deep sigh over the long gone poetry collecting system. He lamented,

Poetry collecting officials,
Listen and collect songs for guidance.
Blame not the speaker but be warned by his words,

下流上通上下泰。
周灭秦兴至隋氏，
十代采诗官不置。
……
君不见：厉王胡亥之末年，

群臣有利君无利。
君兮君兮愿听此：
欲开壅蔽达人情，
先向歌诗求讽刺。

天下有道，这个道，与克己复礼的礼，在内涵上是一致的。

Communication between ranks makes a nation good.

From the Zhou to the Qin and the Sui dynasties,

No officials gathered poetry for ten generations.

...

Did you not behold the debacles of the waning Zhou and Qin,

Ministers raked in gains but the emperor was blindsided.

Gentlemen, oh, gentlemen listen to this,

If you want to demolish the barrier and discover the world,

First turn to poetry and songs with a satirical tone.

The "right principles" mentioned in the saying "when right principles of government prevail in the kingdom, one will show himself" accords with the meaning of "propriety" as per the Confucian injunction "subdue one's self and return to propriety".